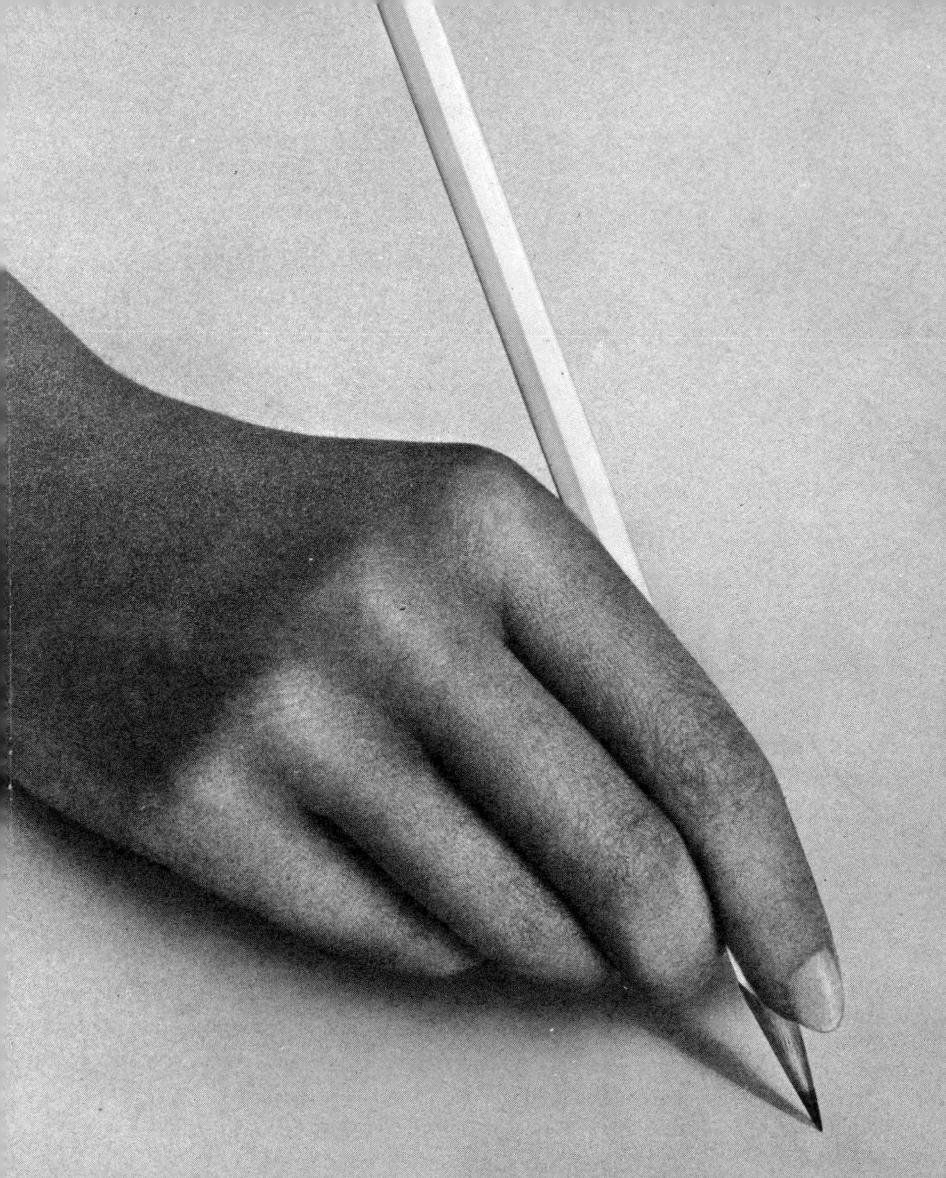

Speedwriting

A B C SHORTHAND ®

COLLEGE EDITION

BOOK THREE

NOTICE

You are now studying a course in *"Speedwriting"* which identifies the best known and, in our opinion, the most efficient system of ABC shorthand. It is known throughout the United States and abroad under the distinguishing trademark and service mark *"Speedwriting."*

"Speedwriting" is the registered trademark and service mark of Speedwriting Publishing Company, Inc., and identifies the books and publications and systems of instruction and teaching of that organization.

Speedwriting
SHORTHAND

COLLEGE EDITION

Simultaneously published in Canada

SIXTH PRINTING

ITT Educational Services, Inc.
55 West 42 Street
New York, New York 10036

Speedwriting shorthand is presently taught in 28 countries and is available in 8 languages:

ENGLISH	PORTUGUESE
FRENCH	GERMAN
SPANISH	FLEMISH
ITALIAN	AFRIKAANS

Shorthand Plates Written by Verleigh Ernest

PRINTED IN THE UNITED STATES OF AMERICA
ISBN 0–8455–0000–7

Lesson 14

You have already learned several sounds that are represented by marks of punctuation. Here is another.

RULE 38 | **For the initial and final sound of "st" write a comma (,).**

Study these examples:

just	**best**
most	**cost**
must	**costs**
first	**insists**
fast	**listings**
trusting	**highest**
largest	**lists**

request		coast	
adjusted		suggests	
biggest		suggested	
tests		guests	

You write:

1. list ____________ 2. chest ____________

3. utmost ____________ 4. requested ____________

5. least ____________ 6. latest ____________

7. lost ____________ 8. past ____________

9. trust ____________ 10. earliest ____________

11. lowest ____________ 12. last ____________

13. listed ____________ 14. contests ____________

15. exist ____________ 16. suggesting ____________

Confirmation:

1. 2. 3. 4.
5. 6. 7. 8.
9. 10. 11. 12.
13. 14. 15. 16.

Note that the rule instructs you to write a comma to indicate the sound of "st." In this connection, pronounce the following pairs of words: *past, passed; mist, missed; baste, based*. You can hear that these words all end with the same sound—the sound of "st." Therefore, since you write a comma for the sound of "st," **passed** is written p, ; **missed** m, ; **based** ba, .

You write:

1. expressed ______ **2. introduced** ______

3. reduced ______ **4. released** ______

5. discussed ______ **6. promised** ______

7. addressed ______ **8. increased** ______

Confirmation.

1. xP, 2. nTdu, 3. rdu, 4. rle, 5. dsc, 6. pm, 7. aD, 8. nCe,

This rule states that a comma is also to be written for the initial sound of "st." To avoid confusion this initial comma must be joined to the rest of outline. For ease in writing it will be raised above the line ______. Thus: **steps** ______ ; **style** ______ ; **stand** ______.

Study these examples:

state ______ **studied** ______

students ______ **still** ______

station ______ **statement** ______

steel ______ **standing** ______

stay ______ **step** ______

You write:

1. staff ____________ **2. stocks** ____________

3. stamped ____________ **4. stated** ____________

5. steam ____________ **6. steady** ____________

7. stands ____________ **8. study** ____________

Confirmation:

1. 2. 3. 4.

5. 6. 7. 8.

Read these sentences:

1.

2.

3.

Key:

1. **We trust that the students who studied passed the first tests.**
2. **Our company is still hoping that the cost of oil can be reduced at least 5 percent.**
3. **If you insist on fast service, we must request that you state your choice of style and color.**

The rule above instructs you to write a comma for the initial and final sound of "st." But what of this sound in the middle of a word? The next rule explains this.

RULE 39 | For the sound of medial "st," write *s* .

In other words, instead of writing a comma for "st" as you do at the beginning or end of a word, you simply write *s* for this sound when it occurs in the middle of a word.

Study these examples:

assistant	*ass-*	**suggestions**	*sjsjs*
statistics	*stscs*	**investments**	*nvs--*
system	*ssm*	**instead**	*nsd*
domestic	*dmsc*	**install**	*nsal*
justly	*jsl*	**installation**	*nsly*
mistake	*msc*	**institute**	*nstu*

You write:

1. institutions ________ **2. estimate** ________

3. installments ________ **4. custom** ________

5. plastic ________ **6. constant** ________

Confirmation:

1. *nstjs* 2. *esma* 3. *nsl--* 4. *csm*
5. *psc* 6. *ks-*

The following words illustrate how the handling of the initial and final sounds of "st" differs from the medial sound of "st."

Study these words:

post	po,	**costs**	c,,
posts	po,,	**costly**	csl
posting	po,	**adjust**	aj,
posted	po,	**adjustments**	ajs--
postal	psl	**state**	,a
postage	psj	**estate**	esa
invest	nv,	**assist**	as,
investment	nvs-	**assists**	as,,
investigate	nvsga	**assistants**	ass--
investigation	nvsgj	**stand**	,—
cost	c,	**newsstand**	nzs—

Now, a final rule for this lesson. Again, you are going to deal with a combination sound – the sound that is derived from the blending together of the sounds of "n" and "k" into "nk."

RULE 40 | **For the sound of "nk," write** g .

This is the sound that is heard in the word *bank*. Since you are to write *q* for the sound of "nk," **bank** is written bq and, in the same way, **think** lq .

You write:

1. pink ______________ **2. thank** ______________

3. banking ______________ **4. tank** ______________

5. blank ______________ **6. ink** ______________

7. delinquent ______________ **8. banquet** ______________

9. blanket ______________ **10. frankly** ______________

11. shrink ______________ **12. thinking** ______________

Confirmation:

1. pq 2. lq 3. bq 4. lq
5. bq 6. iq 7. dlq- 8. bql
9. bql 10. fql 11. Sq 12. lq

Brief Forms

stop	so	**small**	sma
extra	X	**country**	c/
extraordinary	Xo	**always**	l-
real, really	rl	**already**	lr

Abbreviations

capital	Cap	**federal**	fed
represent, representative	rep		
government	gvl		

Additional Words

forced	f,	**outstanding**	ous—=
forecast	fc,	**understand**	Us—
kindest	ci,	**understanding**	Us—=
finest	fi,	**misunderstanding**	-sUs—=
greatest	g,	**understood**	Usd
smaller	sra/	**represents**	reps
smallest	sra,	**representing**	rep
realize	rlz	**represented**	rep
realized	rlz	**representatives**	reps
countries	c//	**stops**	2os
		noticed	nl,

Dictation Hints

To express round numbers above 90, write as follows:

hundred	H	**thousand**	Td
million	⌒	**billion**	B

Examples:

50,000 men	50 Td m		
two million women	2 M wm		
5,000 copies	5 Td cpes	**14 billion**	14 B
$123,000,000	123 Md	**700 books**	7 H bcs

Reading Exercises

1. dM gol; du .	+ wm sde .
p, 5 ys. no v	slscs + sjsjs
Ss v r raq as	Su b r sf v
nCe, O 5 H pc\ l	x pls l, y" yf
as bk . Lj, sl	ur lg v sc ne
pbj v ls ci n .	nvs-- n eT
c/ + subs r	scs o gol
K n a . ra v	b— — e sj,
ab a Td a d\	la u F, so a
ba, o a rs- sde	u nzs— lpc
e esa la a	p. la, Su v
le, a M m	lh v pop raq\

eno la rd l l
hp u nv; u cap
vzl \ l sls f 1,
1d a cpe \ ul
2. ds: las l-b
r cs ldu r
ulso, l nosga
+ sll al—cas
gcl \ las, us
n rc f, pa-
o u —ca ⊙ e
n, F, ns, la
u da p a l,
So . es rā vlu
v. alcls l, vn
fr dSy u ho \\
ino ul Us—
y e cn ps' u
—ca ul lh

za-s n r
h— — \ s
3. 1: vn v hpe
las/ u rq, f
nfy ab ∩
F \\ ∩ F 3
zl a zd- a. za
cly vn e —py
h n r F du
s s/ vcys \
af fnS scl ⊙
h jyn r zf 3
a ass- l .
mf v r akl
dpl + z rpāl
prō l a pzl
v hu, l, \ El l,
y⊙ hz nS-l n
nslu a ful

ssn la sō us
Tds v dl// lz
so efS- la las
lr b nT du, nl
al r rynl
ofss i Fgl
ble h lb a v
Hd [illegible] + a
no, Xo n-
cfl gi kfd-
la hl b a rl
asl l ne nsly
h repo su
4. d [illegible] bg: r u
gl. no, ou v
u ol he ssn?
dzl 2 p U
ks- [illegible] us?
n, u Fz-l cl

u Svsn- Lsc
csl ajs--? r u
f, lpa hl pss
eC y n O lcp
l o sa p el ??
y ku lb dssaT
n u c gl. b,
he ssn o.
Acl f a rlvl
sra asl v
me ?? cf ul
fl ou. bg
Cd la s ncz
el s— l v r
reps l u ho h
l esra. c, v
a kpel nu
nsly + l lso
xpn y l l b

5.

6.

b if sC s .
cas u Sd v k
n + dsc, l
us\ if rdu,pa--
l hp u a al
uv nl bu lus
n . psy Je
env la s ncz\
cu
7. dB: lq u f

u kb1 bv f—
rz di \ a rse
lb s- n a fu
ds \\ z rq; n
u L er lso
s— 4 lcls br
c/ —cb dn/
vC s b hl o
aq9 \ vlu

Key To Lesson 14

1. Dear Mr. Gold: During the past five years, the number of sales of our magazine has increased over 500[2] percent. It has become the largest selling publication of its kind in the country, and subscriptions are coming[4] in at the rate of about a thousand a day. Based on a recent study, we estimate that at least a[6] million men and women studied the statistics and suggestions issued by our staff of experts last year. (¶) If you[6] are thinking of making any investments in either stocks or government bonds, we suggest that you first stop at[10] your newsstand to pick up the latest issue of this very popular magazine. We know that reading it will[12] help you invest your capital wisely. It sells for just $1 a copy. Yours truly, *(136 words)*

2. Dear Sir: It has always been our custom to do our utmost to investigate and settle all claims quickly. To[2] assist us in making fast payment on your claim, we must first insist that you draw up a list showing the estimated[4] value of the articles lost when fire destroyed your home. (¶) I know you will understand why we cannot process[6] your claim until this statement is in our hands. Sincerely, *(70 words)*

3. Gentlemen: I am very happy to answer your request for information about Mr. Front. (¶) Mr. Front[2] was still a student at the state college when we employed him in our firm during his summer vacations. After[4] finishing school, he joined our staff as an assistant to the Manager of our Accounting Department and was[6] rapidly promoted to a position of highest trust. Early last year, he was instrumental in instituting[8] a filing system that saved us thousands of dollars. It was so efficient that it has already been[10] introduced into all our regional offices. (¶) I frankly believe him to be a very hard[12] worker and a most extraordinary man. I feel quite confident that he will be a real asset to any institution[14] he represents. Sincerely yours, *(147 words)*

4. Dear Mr. Blank: Are you getting the most out of your old heating system? Does it stand up under constant winter[2] use? Must you frequently call your serviceman to make costly adjustments? Are you forced to pay higher prices each[4] year in order to keep it operating properly? (¶) Why continue to be dissatisfied when you can get[6] the best heating system on the market for a relatively small amount of money? (¶) If you will fill out the[8] blank card that is enclosed, we will send one of our representatives to your home. He will estimate the cost of[10] a completely new installation and will also explain why it will be worth your while to deal with a company[12] like ours. Yours very truly, *(125 words)*

5. Dear Customer: As I stated in the letter addressed to you last week, dealers from coast to coast are reporting[2] that our new plastic blanket covers are selling better than ever. (¶) In view of this increase in sales, I think it[4] might be wise for you to order some extra covers this month. We still have a large stock in blue, pink, and white; but they[6] are going fast and should be ordered within a week or two. (¶) To prevent any misunderstanding, please make certain[8] that your order states both the style and color you want. Yours truly, *(92 words)*

6. Dear Mr. Flood: Your credit standing at our bank has always been extremely excellent. Therefore, I am really[2] at a loss to understand why your payments have been so delinquent during the past few months. (¶) I realize that[4] something may have happened to prevent your paying these installments on time, but if such is the case, you should have come[6] in and discussed it with us. If reduced payments will help you at all, you have only to write to us in the[8] postage-free envelope that is enclosed. Cordially yours, *(89 words)*

7. Dear Member: Thank you for your contribution to our fund-raising drive. A receipt will be sent in a few days. (¶) As[2] requested in your letter, we are also sending four tickets to our country club dinner,which is being held[4] on August 9. Very truly yours, *(46 words)*

TO PHRASE OR NOT TO PHRASE?

You've come a long way toward mastering *Speedwriting* shorthand. But along the way, have you become a student who phrases excessively? Do you have the mistaken belief that phrasing is the key to shorthand speed? Then take heed.

Excessive phrasing may actually be slowing you down! If you pause for even a fraction of a second in writing a phrase, you have lost speed. A phrase is valuable only when it can be written without the slightest hesitation and can be read accurately. It will help you to remember this.

The Reading Exercises contain phrases such as I will (*il*), he is (*hs*), you can (*uc*), to know (*tno*), and to me (*tme*). In addition to such combinations, it is often possible to omit one or more unimportant words in a common expression. Here are some examples:

nevertheless *nvl'*

time to time *tltm*

more and more *roro*

again and again *agag*

now and then *nvtn*

up to date *pda*

Phrase only those combinations which come to you naturally when you are taking dictation – and only those which occur over and over again. If you have the feeling that you should be phrasing more, forget it! Concentrate on moving from one outline to another with no hesitation!

Writing Assignment—Lesson 14

1. During the past year I investigated the filing systems used by at least a hundred of the largest companies in the country. Based on the statistics I gathered, I frankly think that ours is the least costly and the most efficient.

2. At the request of your representative, we have already sent you an extra copy of our latest price list and style catalog.

3. I really cannot understand why you state that July 28 is the earliest date on which you can install the plastic tank in our plant.

4. Do you want expert suggestions concerning the investment of your capital in stocks and bonds? If so, then stop in at our bank and let one of our staff help you.

5. The Federal Government has just released news of a highway program that will cost several million dollars.

6. Thousands of our customers have already told us that our latest car is the finest model we have ever introduced on the domestic market.

Lesson 15

In previous lessons, you learned that when a word ends in the sound of a long vowel followed by "t," "v," or "m," the long vowel is written to represent the resulting sound. Thus, **gate** *ga* ; **gave** *ga* ; **game** *ga* . You are now going to learn another family of words in which the long vowel will be used in the same way.

RULE 41	**For the final sound of a long vowel and "'r" write the long vowel to represent the resulting sound.**

You can see how similar this rule is to the ones just reviewed regarding the sounds of a long vowel and "t," "v," or "m."

In the following words, notice that the long vowel is written to represent the complete sound of the long vowel + "r."

Study these examples:

dear
here
hearing
engineer
appear
inquire
wire
wiring
tire

desire
desired
require
more
nor
explore
secure
insured
brochure

You write:

1. hear ______ 2. near ______
3. appeared ______ 4. cashier ______
5. fear ______ 6. severe ______
7. acquired ______ 8. entire ______
9. required ______ 10. door ______
11. floor ______ 12. sure ______
13. assured ______ 14. assure ______
15. insure ______ 16. secured ______

Confirmation:

1.	he	2.	ne	3.	apē	4.	cSe
5.	fe	6.	sve	7.	agī	8.	nle
9.	rgī	10.	do	11.	Fo	12.	Su
13.	aSū	14.	aSu	15.	nSu	16.	scū

What of the sound of the vowel in the words *care* or *fair?* This is not the long "a" sound that is heard in *cape* or *fate,* and it is not the short sound of "a" that occurs in the words *cap* or *cat*. In other words, the pronunciation of *a* in *care* and *fair* lies midway between the long- and short-vowel sounds. For the purpose of this rule, however, this sound of "air" will be treated the same way as the other long-vowel sounds and "r."

Study these examples:

fair	fa	**sharing**	Sa̲
care	ca	**fares**	fas
repair	rpa	**aware**	a⌣a
wear	⌣a	**compared**	kpā
hardware	Hd⌣a	**preparing**	ppa̲

You write:

1. chair ________________ **2. prepared** ________________

3. prepare ________________ **4. wearing** ________________

5. bear ______________ 6. share ______________

7. comparing ______________ 8. glare ______________

Confirmation:

1. Ca 2. ppā 3. ppa 4. ⌣a̲
5. ba 6. Sa 7. kpa̲ 8. —ga

Of course, although this rule refers to the final sound of a long vowel + "r," it will be applied when a suffix is added to a root word that is written according to this rule.

Study these words:

clearness	—ce'	nearest	ne,
clearly	—cel	surely	Sul
clearer	—ce/	fairly	fal
careless	cal'	tours	tus
carelessness	cal"	retirement	rtu–
shares	Sas	requirements	rqu––
chairman	Ca⌢–	repairs	rpas

You write:

1. fairness ______________ 2. fearless ______________

3. clearest ______________ 4. nearer ______________

5. dearer ______________ 6. nearly ______________

7. merely ____________ 8. entirely ____________

9. requirement ____________ 10. chairs ____________

11. requires ____________ 12. affairs ____________

Confirmation:

1. fa' 2. fel' 3. —ce, 4. ne/

5. de/ 6. nel 7. ~el 8. nlil

9. rqi– 10. Cas 11. rqis 12. afas

Here's a hint to help you remember the four rules that concern the dropping of a consonant after a long vowel. In the early days of television, a well-known comedian was called Mr. TV. Remember the name. It will remind you that when a word ends in the sound of a long vowel + "m," "r," "t," or "v," only the vowel is written.

Read the following sentences:

1. h z so la n ari ho la ι z Su s h hpn \

2. ι dlī he la . clj ga a dn f . bys o . le \

3. e ble la u dd n gv us . ri na v . njne \

Key:

1. **He was so late in arriving home that I was sure something had happened.**
2. **I am delighted to hear that the college gave a dinner for the boys on the team.**
3. **We believe that you did not give us the right name of the engineer.**

RULE 42 | **Omit n before the sounds of "g," "j," and "ch."**

This rule simply tells you that in such words as *young* or *single,* you will omit the *n* from the outline and write **young** yq and **single** sgl .

Similarly, the *n* will be omitted before the sound of "j," and you will write **singe** sj ; **arrangement** arj- ; **exchange** xCj .

Finally, the rule refers to the sound of "n" before "ch" and, once again, you are to omit the *n*. Thus, **branch** bC ; **franchise** fCz .

Study these words:

luncheon	lCn	**ranch**	rC
thing	lq	**wrong**	rq
long	lq	**strongly**	Sgl
youngsters	yqSs	**among**	amq
passenger	psj	**strangely**	Sjl
arrange	arj	**arranged**	arj̄

You write:

1. branches ____________ 2. lunch ____________

3. along ____________ 4. things ____________

5. longer ____________ 6. bring ____________

7. strong ____________ 8. stronger ____________

9. bringing ______________ **10. arranging** ______________

11. arrangements ______________ **12. younger** ______________

Confirmation:

1. bCs 2. lC 3. alq 4. lgs
5. lg 6. bq 7. Sq 8. Sg
9. bq 10. arj 11. arj-- 12. yg

Note: The outlines for the words *strength* and *length* are derived from the words **strong** Sq and **long** lq ; therefore **strength** Sgl and **length** lgl .

Before going on to the next rule, let's review something you have already learned. You know that for the initial sound of "pl," you write p as in **plan** pn and **play** pa . You also know that for the sound of medial "pl," you write p as in **duplicate** dpca and **apply** api . Similarly, for the sound of initial "bl," you write b as in **blue** bu ; but for medial "bl," you write b as in **problem** pb . The next rule deals with a sound that is closely related to the sounds of "bl" and "pl."

RULE 43	**For the sounds of final "bul" and "blee," write b ; for the sounds of final "pul" and "plee," write p .**

Let's start with the sounds in the words *able, available,* and *possible.* Each of these words contains the final sound of "bul" and, since you are to write *b* for this sound, you write **able** ab ; **available** avlb ; **possible** psb .

The first part of the rule also instructs you to write b for the final sound of "blee." Therefore, **reasonably** rznb ; **possibly** psb .

Study these words:

valuable	vlub	**trouble**	Tb
double	db	**reliable**	rlib
enable	nab	**favorable**	fvb
suitable	sub	**favorably**	fvb
profitably	pflb	**reasonable**	rznb

You write:

1. table ______ **2. doubly** ______

3. desirable ______ **4. dependable** ______

5. payable ______ **6. eligible** ______

7. enjoyable ______ **8. suitably** ______

Confirmation:

1. tb 2. db 3. dzib 4. dp—b

5. pab 6. —ejb 7. njyb 8. sub

The second part of the rule states that *p* is to be written for the final sound of "pul" or "plee."

Study these words:

example	*xp*	**simple**	*sp*
people	*pp*	**simply**	*sp*
couple	*cp*	**examples**	*xps*

Brief Forms

open	*op*	**result**	*rsl*
opinion	*opn*	**important**	*ip*
life	*lf*	**between**	*bl*
prove	*pv*	**subject**	*sj*
difficult, difficulty	*dfk*	**situation**	*sil*
regular, regulation, regularly	*reg*		

Abbreviations

establish	*esl*

Additional Words

regulations	*regs*	**established**	*esl̄*
results	*rsls*	**establishing**	*esl̲*

resulting	rsl	establishment	esl-
resulted	rsl	ample	mp
opened	op	amply	mp
opening	op	considerable	ksb
proved	pv	considerably	ksb
proves	pvs	herewith	he
approval	apvl	herein	hen
approved	apv	questionnaire	qa
subjects	sjs	welfare	lfa

Dictation Hints

Express time as follows:

2 o'clock 2° **10 o'clock** 10° **10:30** 10^{30}

Reading Exercises

1. drs Sq: so + so pp r bq l Us— h ep ls f r chn lagi . b, edcj avlb u Su la z a T u Sa lh opn + rlz h nec ls l ppa u yqSs f. fC

rol ly l v l
—pa n. hSe v
r c/ \\ lh nl
sy l b —cel +
Tol dsc, a r
lCn re n fb
b dr h bn
hu s a pop
aT + as lqb
rcgnz z a ld
n s fld \ n
. fed gvl est
a k lnvsga .
pbrs v edcy
lz dr bn hu
z apy= z
Ca— v la k \\
ino s lc l pv
xTel vlub +

c Sgl ry u lb
v us cf psb \
s

2. ds: cs ev
lv l; u arg
r b, Ks e lg
l nl fa la u
b arg. F, lb
lol ab. FnC
s b hl a r bC
S o vd sp 5 \\
f j, lh sgl d
er q lc l psb
f u lpC pess
F r reg x a
. no, rznb
pss n r hSe \
f xp a slv
4 lnl Cas +

a Lj ~C lb
~C Nl c,,
250d lb sol
f nl 175d \ e
nvi u ttc avj
v lh opl \ r~B
r dos r~m op
ul 9° E vn \ su
3. ~d) pl : c
~gl lnf~ u la
er n ppā l
sn a Flz aGe-
v u a lhl \ e
fl la sC a aGe-
d n pv pflb
+ d ~el rsl
n a dfk sil
bl us + r lcl
dl/ \ h~E ~f

ud ca lh—l r
h v Hd~a n
. req ~m ed
b hpe L~c .
nec arj--\ wl
4. dK : h~ lg r
e rqī l ~a
bf e he F~ u?
4 ~ol za-- v
lr gn ou lu
b uv n~s-
us u Cc no
rln lus \ er n
ab L~a ne
lg + v sc r
a ne l bq su
aq u f pa-f.
S- v lrb s
n rsē b. e—

v lh vk \ ul
5. d ℩ yq: ino ur
a va la . cr uv
j, agī reps a
Lj nvs- \ ino(.)
lo(.) la ul lq l
dzib ldu E u
c lgl . b, psb
oG \\ he r s
sp yl cp lgs
uc du la l
nab u l db . lf
v u cr + nSu
la ll gv u
ys v nyyb(.)
Tb(.) Je Svs \
① bq u cr l a
rlib Sp . vo-
s seo lb rq \
do- va ul a
sra ajs- bks
a nf/rpa jb \
② cf pls v ne
cr r rqī(.) x
Su la ly r scū
J a dp— b Ss \
③ flo al nScys
n rGd lreq
sznl Ccps \ ④
lq v us vn und
a nu li o lub \
r b— v q(.) Sq
lis + lubs l n
nl ad l . kfl
v u + u psy//(.)
b l lso gv u .
ad Q-e v a saf
Tp \\ hpe du \ c

Key To Lesson 15

1. Dear Mrs. Strong: More and more people are beginning to understand how important it is for our children to[2] acquire the best education available. I am sure that, as a mother, you share this opinion and[4] realize how necessary it is to prepare your youngsters for the future role they will have to play in the[6] history of our country. (¶) This entire subject will be clearly and thoroughly discussed at our luncheon meeting in[8] February by Dr. H. Brown, who is a popular author and has long been recognized as a leader[10] in his field. When the Federal Government established a committee to investigate the problems of[12] education, it was Dr. Brown who was appointed as chairman of that committee. (¶) I know his talk will prove[14] extremely valuable, and I strongly urge you to be with us if possible. Sincerely, *(156 words)*

2. Dear Madam: Because we have always listed you among our best customers, we think it only fair that you be[2] among the first to be told about the furniture sale being held at our branch store on Wednesday, September 5.[4] (¶) For just this single day, we are going to make it possible for you to purchase pieces from our regular[6] stock at the most reasonable prices in our history. For example, a set of four walnut chairs and a[8] large matching table, which normally costs $250, will be sold for only[10] $175. (¶) We invite you to take advantage of this opportunity. Remember, our doors remain[12] open until 9 o'clock every evening. Sincerely yours, *(136 words)*

3. My dear Mr. Place: I regret to inform you that we are not prepared to sign a franchise agreement with you[2] at this time. We feel that such an agreement would not prove profitable and would merely result in a difficult[4] situation between us and our local dealers. (¶) However, if you would care to handle our line of hardware[6] in the regular manner, we would be happy to make the necessary arrangements. Yours very truly,[8] *(80 words)*

4. Dear Customer: How long are we required to wait before we hear from you? Four monthly statements have already gone[2] out to you, but you have neither sent us your check nor written to us. (¶) We are not able to wait any longer[4] and have asked our attorney to bring suit against you if payment for the shipment of lumber is not received by[6] the end of this week. Yours truly, *(65 words)*

5. Dear Mr. Young: I know you are aware that the car you have just acquired represents a large investment. I know,[2] too, that you will think it desirable to do everything you can to get the best possible operation.[4] (¶) Here are some simple yet important things you can do that will enable you to double the life of your car[6] and insure that it will give you many years of enjoyable, trouble-free service. 1. Bring your car to a[8] reliable shop the moment something seems to be wrong. Don't wait until a small adjustment becomes a major repair[10] job. 2. If parts of any kind are required, make sure that they are secured from a dependable source. 3. Follow[12] all instructions in regard to regular seasonal checkups. 4. Think of us when you need a new tire or tube. Our[14] brand of good, strong tires and tubes will not only add to the comfort of you and your passengers, but will also give[16] you the added guarantee of a safe trip. (¶) Happy driving. Cordially, *(173 words)*

Name..............................Class.........Date................

Writing Assignment – Lesson 15

1. We can assure you that your entire family will enjoy a long vacation on our ranch.

____

____

2. If the results of our questionnaire prove favorable – and we find that many people share your opinion – we may possibly arrange to establish a branch store in the near future.

____

____

____

____

____

3. Are you aware that buying the wrong tires may considerably decrease the life of your car?

____

____

____

4. You will be glad to hear that it is a simple thing to open a regular charge account at our shop.

____

____

5. The enclosed brochure will bring you information on the subject of the important alterations made in our retirement plan.

6. Can you arrange to meet me for lunch between two and three o'clock to discuss the situation that has occurred?

7. I am sure that the chairman of the committee can secure the information he requires from our chief engineer.

BRIEF FORM and STANDARD ABBREVIATION REVIEW

Lessons 11 through 15

1. Dear Mr. Deal: I note from your report that our average monthly sales between June and September are already[2] considerably above those of last year. (¶) Am I correct in assuming that this extraordinary[4] increase is due to the extra advertising we have done in local evening papers? If you really believe[6] that it is, then I think it necessary to invest an even greater part of our capital in this[8] way. Yours truly, *(82 words)*

2. Dear Mrs. Field: I have written to you several times directing your attention to the amount that you still[2] owe us under the terms of our contract. As you know, keeping such a small amount open on our books proves extremely[4] difficult; and it is important that you make payment in full before the end of the month. (¶) Why not send us[6] a check while this letter is before you? Very truly yours, *(70 words)*

3. Dear Friend: Should large steel companies be subject to control by the Federal Government? Should the Government[2] establish maximum prices that may be charged for steel? (¶) Some people subscribe to the opinion that such control is[4] absolutely necessary for the benefit of the public and that it would greatly contribute to the[6] economic life of the country. However, certain representatives of the Government and the steel[8] companies feel that these regulations would not prove satisfactory and would only result in difficult[10] situations. (¶) Both sides of this question are fully discussed in the current issue of the magazine we publish.[12] The magazine always sells rapidly, and we suggest that you stop at your newsstand while copies are still available.[14] Sincerely yours, *(144 words)*

4. Dear Sir: A fire in our shipping department is causing a delay in the delivery of our merchandise,[2] and we estimate that it will take a minimum of 10 days before we can fill your recent order. (¶) We hope[4] you will not only understand the reason for the delay but will also realize that this is a situation[6] that is completely beyond our control. Cordially yours, *(76 words)*

–REVIEW–

Lessons 11 through 15

1. Dear Mr. Frank: Thank you for taking the trouble to arrange the delivery of a courtesy copy of[2] your latest illustrated history book. I have examined it thoroughly and think it compares favorably with[4] the one we have used for such a long time. (¶) Those teachers who have studied its contents had many comments to[6] make on the clear and enjoyable fashion in which the author presents his subject, and they were most emphatic[8] in expressing the opinion that this excellent book would prove valuable in their classes. Personally,[10] I am quite willing to go along with their suggestions and am prepared to place an order provided you can[12] guarantee delivery in ample time for the start of our fall semester. Cordially yours, *(137 words)*

2. Dear Bill: Would it be possible to arrange a luncheon appointment on Friday to discuss further the contract[2] I must sign by July 28? (¶) I still have a great many questions to ask, and I feel you are the only person[4] competent enough to answer them for me. Cordially, *(51 words)*

3. Dear Mrs. Story: I am enclosing the name and address of the dealer in your area who handles our[2] complete line. I am sure that he will be able to recommend the best type of storm windows for your home. Yours truly, *(40 words)*

4. Dear Mr. Steel: I have written you several times in connection with the amount that is still outstanding on[2] your account. (¶) The large assortment of leather boxes shipped on July 6 was sent on credit, and you promised to make[4] payment by the first of the following month. However, we have had no word from you; and we must now insist[6] on settlement of your bill by the end of the week. (¶) If we have not heard from you by then, we will be forced to[8] authorize our attorney to bring suit against you. Won't you help us avoid taking this step by sending your check? Yours[10] very truly, *(102 words)*

—NOTICE—

THE INTERNATIONAL REGISTRATION FORM IS BOUND INTO THE FRONT OF BOOK ONE. IF IT IS MISSING WHEN YOU ARE GIVEN THIS BOOK, OR IF YOU ARE GIVEN THIS FORM ON A SEPARATE SHEET OF PAPER, NOTIFY:

THE SPEEDWRITING COMPANY
55 West 42 Street, New York, N.Y. 10036

Unless this form is filled in by you and registered with the national office in New York City, YOU WILL LOSE ALL LIFE-TIME TRANSFER, BRUSH-UP, AND EMPLOYMENT PRIVILEGES.

ACCEPT NO EXPLANATIONS
OR SUBSTITUTIONS.

More Help For Students

HOW TO DETERMINE THE LENGTH OF A LETTER

In a short time now you'll be on the job as a happy, working secretary – and chances are you'll be able to estimate the length of any letter just at a glance. But until you have had enough experience in this respect, you have to have a definite method of determining the number of words in a letter. Here is the easy way to do this –

Count the number of words in the first three lines of the body of the letter in your shorthand notes. Divide this number by three. You then have the average number of words in each line. Now count the number of lines in your notes and multiply this number by the average number of words in each line. The resulting number is a good estimate of the total number of words in the letter.

For example: If there are 21 words in the first three lines of your notes, divide 21 by 3. This gives you an average of 7 words per line. If there are 20 lines of shorthand, multiply 20 by 7 and you will find that there are approximately 140 words in the body of the letter.

As you become more experienced, you will learn to estimate the length of a letter without counting. If a letter contains 125 words and you have written 1¼ columns, excluding the inside address and salutation, you have written about one hundred words to a column. By checking in this manner over a period of a few days, you will be able to estimate the length of a letter by just looking at the length of your notes.

Lesson 16

Let's start this lesson with a review of the marks of punctuation that you have learned in previous lessons.

1. UNDERSCORE: For "ing" or "thing" that is added to a word: **getting** *gt̲* ; **something** *s_* .
2. OVERSCORE: For "ed" that is added to form the past tense of a word: **named** *nā* ; **required** *rqī* .
3. HYPHEN: For the medial and final sounds of "nt" or "ment": **went** *w-* ; **statement** *2a-* .
4. DASH: for the medial and final sound of "nd": **depend** *dp—* ; **handle** *h—l* .
5. APOSTROPHE: For the final ss and <u>ness</u> : **discuss** *dsc'* ; **happiness** *hpe'*.
6. QUOTATION MARK: For the final <u>ssness</u> : **fearlessness** *fel"* ; **hopelessness** *hopl"* .
7. COMMA: For the initial and final sounds of "st": **first** *F,* ; **discussed** *dsc,* ; **step** *,p* .
8. SLANT (joined): For the final sounds of "er" and "ter": **bigger** *bg/* ; **after** *af/* .

Read the following sentences:

1. e ~, ns, la u s— a L tl̲ us y u rfz ldsc'. ~ v r aj—\

2. ev j, rtn̄ l. ofs af a lq—i' b ~ kfd— la i8 b ab lat— u F, ~e̲ a. e— v. vk\

3. n ~u jj—o u v no rzn lfl sC hopl" n rGd l. ev—— la oc̄ l, ~o\

Key:

1. **We must insist that you send a letter telling us why you refused to discuss the matter with our agent.**
2. **I have just returned to the office after a long illness, but I am confident that I shall be able to attend your first meeting at the end of the week.**
3. **In my judgment, you have no reason to feel such hopelessness in regard to the events that occurred last month.**

You are now going to learn to use another mark of punctuation to represent a sound.

RULE 44 | For the final sound of "tee" write) .

Ordinarily, this mark of punctuation) is called a right parenthesis; but because this is rather a long name, it will be referred to as a blend.

Study these examples:

city	s)	**duty**	du)
safety	sf)	**duties**	du))
maturity	mtu)	**quantity**	q-)
university	unVs)	**authority**	aT)
liberty	lB)	**county**	k)
community	kn)	**quantities**	q-))
facilities	fsl))	**quality**	ql)

You write:

1. beauty __________	**2. locality** __________
3. property __________	**4. security** __________
5. faculty __________	**6. purity** __________
7. party __________	**8. capacity** __________
9. pretty __________	**10. activities** __________
11. qualities __________	**12. cities** __________

Confirmation:

1. bu)	2. lcl)	3. pP)	4. scu)
5. fcl)	6. pu)	7. P)	8. cps)
9. p)	10. acv))	11. ql))	12. s))

Notice in the following words that you retain the root outline and simply add a blend) for the addition of the sound of "tee": **possible** psb ; **possibility** psb) ; **able** ab ; **ability** ab) ; **disability** dsab) ; **necessary** nec ; **necessity** nec) ; **public** pb ; **publicity** pb) ; **popular** pop ; **popularity** pop).

Before going on to the next rule, let's look back at two rules which were in lessons you have already covered. You will recall that **made** is written md and **graze** gz , in accordance with the rules that stated that you are to drop the long vowel when it is followed by the sound of "d" or "z." Thus: **raid** rd ; **raise** rz ; **seed** sd ; **seize** sz ; **wide** wd ; **wise** wz ; **rode** rd ; **rose** rz ; **feud** fd ; **fuse** fz .

The rule which you are now going to learn deals with another group of words in which you will also omit the long vowel and write the consonant sound that follows it.

RULE 45 | **For the sounds of "ane, een, one," and "une" write n ; for the sound of "ine" write in .**

You can see that once again you are going to drop the long vowel and write the consonant sound that follows it.

Study these examples:

gain	gn	**means**	mns
main	mn	**loan**	ln

cleaned	-cn̄	**phone**	fn
green	gn	**noon**	nn
dean	dn	**plain**	-pn

You write:

1. seen ______________ **2. mean** ______________

3. soon ______________ **4. grain** ______________

5. shown ______________ **6. zone** ______________

7. screening ______________ **8. training** ______________

Confirmation:

1. sn 2. mn 3. sn 4. gn
5. Sn 6. zn 7. sCn̲ 8. Tn̲

Notice that this rule refers to the sounds of "ane, een, one," and "une," but it does <u>not</u> include the sound of "ine" that is heard in such words as *sign* and *design*. For this sound of "ine," you will write *in* no matter how many syllables are in the word.

Study these examples:

sign	sin	**incline**	ncin
design	dzin	**assigned**	asin̄
assignment	asin-	**combined**	Kbin̄

You write:

1. decline __________ **2. inclined** __________

3. resign __________ **4. designed** __________

Confirmation:

1. dcin 2. ncin̄ 3. rzin 4. dzin̄

To summarize: When a word contains the sound of a long vowel and "d," "z," or "n," write the consonant and drop the vowel – except for the sound of "ine," for which you write both the *i* and *n*. It may be helpful for you to remember the outline for the clue word **design** dzin. As you look at this outline, say the rule – drop all vowels before *d, z,* and *n,* except for the long *i* before *n*.

One further point before proceeding to the last rule in this lesson. According to the rule, you write **chain** Cn. However, in the words *change, range,* and *strange* an additional rule must be applied–the omission of *n* before *j*. Thus: **change** Cj ; **changes** Cjs ; **range** rj ; **strange** Sj .

RULE 46	For the initial sound of "im" write i ; for the initial sound of "un" write u .

Study these examples:

imprinted	iP=	**unless**	ul'
imperative	iPv	**unfortunately**	ufCnll
impose	ipz	**undoubtedly**	udtl
impossible	ipsb	**unemployment**	upy-
impossibility	ipsb)	**unable**	uab

You write:

1. imprinting ______ 2. unpaid ______

3. imposing ______ 4. unwise ______

5. imitation ______ 6. unskilled ______

7. imitate ______ 8. unlikely ______

9. unhappy ______ 10. unfair ______

Confirmation:

1. iP= 2. upd 3. ipz 4. uz

5. ij 6. uscl̄ 7. ida 8. ulcl

9. uhpe 10. ufa

Brief Forms

whole	hl	acknowledge	ak
develop	dv	almost	lso

organize, organization	og
immediate, immediately	ida
particular, particularly	P
success, successful, successfully	suc

Abbreviations

volume	vol	ounce	oz	pair	pr

Additional Words

wholesale	hls	improve	Ꮯsv
wholesaler	hls/	improving	Ꮯsv̲
acknowledged	ak̄	improvement	Ꮯsv-
acknowledgement	ak-	improvements	Ꮯsv--
developing	dv̲	improved	Ꮯsv̄
development	dv-	unnecessary	unec
developments	dv--	unsatisfactory	usal
developed	dv̄	pairs	prs
confirm	kf	confirmation	kfl

Reading Exercises

1. d/ ga: eap.	v gn h s pa-
Clse Sn lr rep	s lr o. lc +
n h cl̄\. Ou	Sd reC u b.
ga h f 25 glns	e— v. k\ul

2. dbl: w. L
n vC u sc̄
vT dg. ds—
f usct lb l
sv n. fC\ ls
u opn la ll
n(o) + i Y Sgl
sj, la ulc. Tn
Css i j un
e l \\ u udbl
v. nec ab) +
unl ldv a hi
dGe v scl n
lh P fld(o) + ld
b uz l p of
lh Tn ne lg
ln s nec \\ z i
lol u(o) ls a ll
ulcl la ur
Ezb f a xd-
ln 7. bq(o) b
lh dz n nec
m la ecn
suc Vc ou
s_ bl us\ cl
re un a fu
ds so la ec
ary lre + dsc'
lh v\ s

3. ds: n u
cps) z my
v r m ofs(o)
u f, lru lu
ab. r m 185 69
o u akl \\ pa-
o lh ol bl s lq
Odu(o) + e d lc
lo r me\

ls unec lru us
a L⊖ a Cc
lb sfS- \ ul
4. d) bl: El
l, s√ e pC̄
a Lj pes v
p) 7 . s)
gvl f. Pps v
bld a kn) s⌐
f r yq pp\
sfS- f——
v fel b rz̄ ⓡ+
er hop la Uc
l bq ida\ e
esra la kScj
l lc lro a y ⓡ
b s v. fsl))
Sd b rde n
ab 6 ros\\ .

Bs v r oq
vS lak + lq
u f. hp u ga
us\ v Su
ul gn a q dl
v sal 7 .
nlj la u pā
sC a up Pl n
. suc v. hl
pG\ cu
5. d) Sq : z c
xpn̄ o. fn vn
c lc v u ySd ⓡ
e n, sc u l
va a ll lg
f. 12 prs v gol
Sus u rq, o
jl 23\ . vol
v T° as b P

hvl. + e v b
uab lcp p u
. ds — \\ hvE.
r —p- s n
Uc= Ol; + lz
Sus Sd sn b
avlb n vlE
g-) una dzi \
vlu

6. ds: er n
rse v u ur
n vCu Ō
10 dzn 12Θ oz
pp klnl/ vP=
u . na + aD'
v u S \\ e rlz
la ls vPo f u
lgl lz klnl/
gcl. b ls

cpsb lS ls ul
uv —cn p u
upd bl \ ul'
u Cc reCs us
sn. eS b f,
ldcn al F
Os 7s u \\ lu
—p ak lh nl
u u Cc \ lg
u \ ul

7. d) Vc: v u
ks vl d hpn
cf a fzcl dsab)
o upy-pa
sdn 20 l u
nk?? z a F.
rT ln a af-.
w l fel l
u du) lrc

ary--f. plcy
v u vrf +
chn + la s y
u sC a F
ble/ n. plses
iSū b. co i
rep\ lz plses
r dzn lgv u
. scu) v no
la pa--l l
b avlb f
dcl bls +
h shol nds ||
u lc. lB)
v fl d a
bcll la dsc".
vd ry v plses
e c pvd\ n
al fa' l u

fsl u Sd
rd. bcll v
q ca\ ul
8. d) sno: w
y, sn dn
bn + v d
l-v ary--f r
og luz. fsl))
v. unVs) f r
—cbs acv))
ls fal + v-l\
ufCnll h E
l s a psb) la
ll b nec lG
. da v r Xs
P) cs a ip
2d- + fcl)
e s scdē
f la P nu +

cn b csl̄ l
akda us\\ i
l fn u 1, 3
sn 3 aT da
asb sl \ su

Key to Lesson 16

1. Dear Mr. Gray: We appreciate the courtesy shown to our representative when he called. (¶) The order you[2] gave him for 25 gallons of green house paint is already on the truck and should reach you by the end of the[4] week. Yours truly, *(42 words)*
2. Dear Bill: I have the letter in which you asked whether I think the demand for unskilled labor will improve in the[2] future. It is my opinion that it will not, and I therefore strongly suggest that you take the training courses[4] I mentioned when we met. (¶) You undoubtedly have the necessary ability and intelligence to develop[6] a high degree of skill in this particular field, and it would be unwise to put off this training any[8] longer than is necessary. (¶) As I told you, it is a little unlikely that you are eligible[10] for a student loan from the bank; but this does not necessarily mean that we cannot successfully work out[12] something between us. Call me within a few days so that we can arrange to meet and discuss this matter. Sincerely,[14] *(140 words)*
3. Dear Sir: In my capacity as manager of our main office, I am forced to write to you about the remaining[2] $185.69 on your account. (¶) Payment on this old bill is long[4] overdue, and we would like to have our money. It is unnecessary to write us a letter – a check will be[6] sufficient. Yours truly, *(64 words)*
4. Dear Mr. Billings: Early last summer we purchased a large piece of property from the city government for[2] the purpose of building a community center for our young people. Sufficient funds have finally been raised,[4] and we are hoping that work will begin immediately. We estimate that construction will take almost a[6] year, but some of the facilities should be ready in about six months. (¶) The members of our organization[8] wish to acknowledge and thank you for the help you gave us. I am sure you will gain a great deal of satisfaction[10] from the knowledge that you played such an important part in the success of the whole program. Cordially yours, *(126 words)*

5. Dear Mr. Strong: As I explained on the phone when I talked with you yesterday, we must ask you to wait a little[2] longer for the 12 pairs of gold shoes you requested on July 23. The volume of orders has been[4] particularly heavy, and we have been unable to keep up with the demand. (¶) However, our plant is now[6] working overtime; and these shoes should soon be available in whatever quantity you may desire. Very[8] truly yours, *(81 words)*

6. Dear Sir: We are in receipt of your wire in which you ordered 10 dozen 12-ounce paper containers imprinted[2] with the name and address of your store. (¶) We realize that it is imperative for you to get these containers[4] quickly, but it is impossible to ship them until you have cleaned up your unpaid bill. Unless your check reaches[6] us soon, we shall be forced to decline all further orders from you. (¶) Will you please acknowledge this note with your check. Thank[8] you. Yours truly, *(82 words)*

7. Dear Mr. Bright: Have you considered what would happen if a physical disability or unemployment[2] put a sudden stop to your income? (¶) As a father, rather than an agent, I have always felt it my duty to make[4] arrangements for the protection of my wife and children; and that is why I am such a firm believer[6] in the policies issued by the company I represent. These policies are designed to give you the[8] security of knowing that payments will always be available for medical bills and household needs. (¶) I[10] am taking the liberty of forwarding a booklet that discusses the wide range of policies we can[12] provide. In all fairness to your family, you should read the booklet with great care. Yours truly, *(135 words)*

8. Dear Mr. Snow: I have just seen Dean Brown and have made tentative arrangements for our organization to use[2] the facilities of the university for our club's activities this fall and winter. Unfortunately,[4] however, there is a possibility that it will be necessary to change the date of

our Christmas[6] party because an important student and faculty meeting is scheduled for that particular night and[8] cannot be canceled to accommodate us. (¶) I will phone you just as soon as another date has been set. Sincerely[10] yours, *(102 words)*

Writing Assignment—Lesson 16

1. The report I was shown indicates the possibility that the City Council will organize a committee to study unemployment problems in this particular community.

2. Will you please phone our office as soon as possible if the quality of service does not improve.

3. Unless there is a change in this unsatisfactory condition, we will face the necessity of assigning our publicity to another firm.

4. Unfortunately, I am unable to attend the party being given by the Dean for the members of the University's faculty.

5. We have successfully developed a new engine that combines all the features of safety and beauty that our customers demand.

6. Although you acknowledged receipt of my letter almost two weeks ago, I have heard nothing in regard to the request I made for a loan. May I know whether my request was declined?

Lesson 17

RULE 47 | **In words of more than one syllable, write X for the medial and final sounds of "us, usly, shus, shusly, shul, shully, nshul, nshully."**

Let's examine this rule carefully. It states that *x* is to be written for the sounds of "us" and "usly." Therefore, **obvious** and **obviously** are written obvx. In the same way, **generous** and **generously** jnrx; **previous** and **previously** pvx.

Study these examples:

campus	cmpx	**numerous**	nmrx
surplus	Spx	**tremendous**	Tm—x
bonus	bnx	**tremendously**	Tm—x
bonuses	bnxs	**famous**	fax
religious	rljx	**famously**	fax

You write:

1. courteous ________ **2. courteously** ________

3. devious ________ **4. status** ________

5. monotonous ________ **6. desirous** ________

Confirmation:

1. Clx 2. Clx 3. dvx 4. slx

5. mtnx 6. dzrx

This rule also tells you to write *x* for the sounds of "shus" and "shusly." Therefore, you write **anxious** and **anxiously** agx ; **conscious** and **consciously** kx **delicious** dlx ; **ambitious** abx .

You write:

1. precious ________ **2. graciously** ________

Confirmation:

1. px 2. gx

This rule also instructs you to write *x* for the sounds of "shul" and "shully." Thus, **beneficial** bnfx ; **commercial** and **commercially** kx ; **partial** px ; **social** and **socially** sx ; **official** and **officially** ofx ; **officials** ofxs .

And finally, the rule refers to the sound of "nshul" and "nshully" and you are instructed to write *x* for these sounds. Observe how this is done in the following words.

Study these examples:

confidential	kfdx	**financial**	fnx
confidentially	kfdx	**financially**	fnx
essential	esx	**credentials**	cdxs
essentially	esx	**residential**	rzdx

RULE 48	**For the medial and final sound of a vowel followed by "ry" write** y **.**

In other words, you are to write *y* for the sounds of "ary, ery, iry, ory," and "ury." Observe how this rule is followed in these words.

Study these examples:

salary	sly	**sorry**	sy
temporary	tmpy	**hurry**	hy
stationery	sty	**territory**	try
worry	wy	**inventory**	nv-y
inquiry	nqy	**weary**	wy

You write:

1. military ________________ **2. carry** ________________

3. voluntary ________________ **4. library** ________________

5. machinery ________________ **6. customary** ________________

7. preliminary ______________ 8. ordinary ______________

9. memory ______________ 10. summary ______________

Confirmation:

1. slly 2. cy 3. vl-y 4. lBy
5. sBny 6. csny 7. plmy 8. odny
9. my 10. smy

Notice that the rule states that you are to write *y* also for the medial sounds of "ary, ery, iry, ory," and "ury." Therefore, **material** mtyl ; **series** syz ; **serious** syx ; **period** pyd ; **various** vyx ; **interior** ntyr ; **editorial** edtyl .

RULE 49	For the sound of "sp," write a small printed s .

You have learned to print a capital *S* for the sound of "str." This rule instructs you to write a small printed *s* for the sound of "sp" whenever it occurs in a word.

Study these examples:

speed	sd	**speak**	sec
spend	s—	**spare**	sa
hospital	hstl	**inspection**	nscj
prospective	pscv	**specifications**	ssfcjs
specific	ssfc	**grasping**	gs

clasped	—cS̄	**special**	Sx
speech	seC	**especially**	eSx

Read the following sentences:

1. hw mC m, i s— f. Sa
tr f mi cr?

2. wn i sec l. mnj̄o il ll
h la u v iSu Ssfc nScys
f. nScy v. hsll.

Key:

1. **How much must I spend for the spare tire for my car?**
2. **When I speak to the manager, I will tell him that you have issued specific instructions for the inspection of the hospital.**

You write:

1. spite ____________	**2. spot** ____________
3. spent ____________	**4. space** ____________
5. inspector ____________	**6. spending** ____________
7. speaker ____________	**8. spoke** ____________
9. dispose ____________	**10. inspire** ____________

Confirmation:

1. Si 2. Sl 3. S- 4. Sas

5. 6. 7. 8.

9. 10.

As you know, the initial sounds of "br, pr, gr," etc., are expressed by writing an initial hyphen on the first letter of the outline. For the sound of "spr" at the beginning of a word, do the same: . Thus, **spread** and **spring** . Similarly, "spl" at the beginning of a word is written with an initial dash: . Thus, **splice** and **splendid** .

Again recalling a rule that has already been covered, you will treat the sound of medial "spl" as you do the medial sound of "bl" or "gl" – that is, you will eliminate the initial dash and write only the printed *s*. Thus, **display** .

One further point before leaving this rule. What of words such as *sport* or *sparse?* These will be handled as you do any sound that is followed by a medial vowel + "r" – that is, you capitalize the preceding letter – in this case printed *s*. Therefore, **sport** ; **spirit** ; **sparse** .

Brief Forms

thought	**poor**
around	**idea**
world	**object**
usual, usually	**initial, initially**
probable, probably	**definite, definitely**

Abbreviations

minute		warehouse	
junior		senior	
manufacture		independent	
signature		America, American	
approximate, approximately			

Additional Words

manufacturing		ideas	
manufacturer		ideal	
manufacturers		probability	
manufactured		unusual	
objective		minutes	
objection		continuous	
directory		continuously	

Reading Exercises

1. drs ral: .
ob v lhL sl
ll u ab.
Z— x nv-y
s la er hol a
r — E sl
hs o fb 27\
v . 3q szn so
—cos a h— (2)
er esx agx l
rc sas f r
nu le (;) + er (2)
Z/ (2) of— fMx
diss O r nle
xc \\ lh s no
odny s\ . d"
ul se o dsa
v pC f
Co fax fr/

v ms —col (1)
+ lyx sl f ksb
so ln er sc\
u — a Sl
d' o a sofil
oufl f vn va (3)
ul fe l he\\ y
n lc a fu
ns lk n+
lc r \ ul

2. d bgs: w
f, sn . ind
Sva rd b u
k o. po gl)
lb f — n
Sln rdse cy
n vyx lcl So\\
lg s v u
Cgs r x el syx (2)

+ i Sgl -uj u l
sec -u a^ne
bf u du ne dfn
ab -u id lpb
-u fi \ ifl Su
la hl b ncin
laGe la pbj v
lh rSl d pb
rsl n lgl
acj aq u \\ -p
ll -re no
-l u dsd ldu\
vlu

3. ds: -n i soc
- u o nv 3
-d l qi -pn
la lz abs esx
f. -lyl e O
lb dē no la

ln ja 13\ u sd
l d lc a pyd
v apx 2 -ros
l-c lh P S-\\
ls n- ja 6
+ er bq l -y
cs ev rsē; nl
Px S-o lh O\
zi lol u a
dla v -n a
sgl d d rsl
n a q fnx l'
lr F + e d
ap -u du -lE
s nec l sd lh
S- alg\\ er Su
u Us— la -u
ab) l h—l lh
ix O l d^m r

fC rlyS \ ul
4. ds: lh s n
rpi l u ngy
v ag 4 n vC
u sc̄ ab . sx
Css op l m
hu r zj a .
llly hsll \\
n pv+ ys r
unVs) of a
syz v sC Css
+ plmy
ary-- r nv
b d ldu . sa
lh y \ allo a
kpe sy v
sys s n yl
rde er lro
Sln la el rpe

r Cs n a
hSe cs l pv
so pop l,
s S \ n 2x
m hu lc .
Cs d a dfn
py- v ll us
no h C
ly h njj l \\
uf ud lc l
s— s v u
Sa h lc / v
r —s—d Css
uv nl yl ou
. apcy bq
la s ncz \ no
Ssfc rqi--
r nec + no
Cq s d f bcs

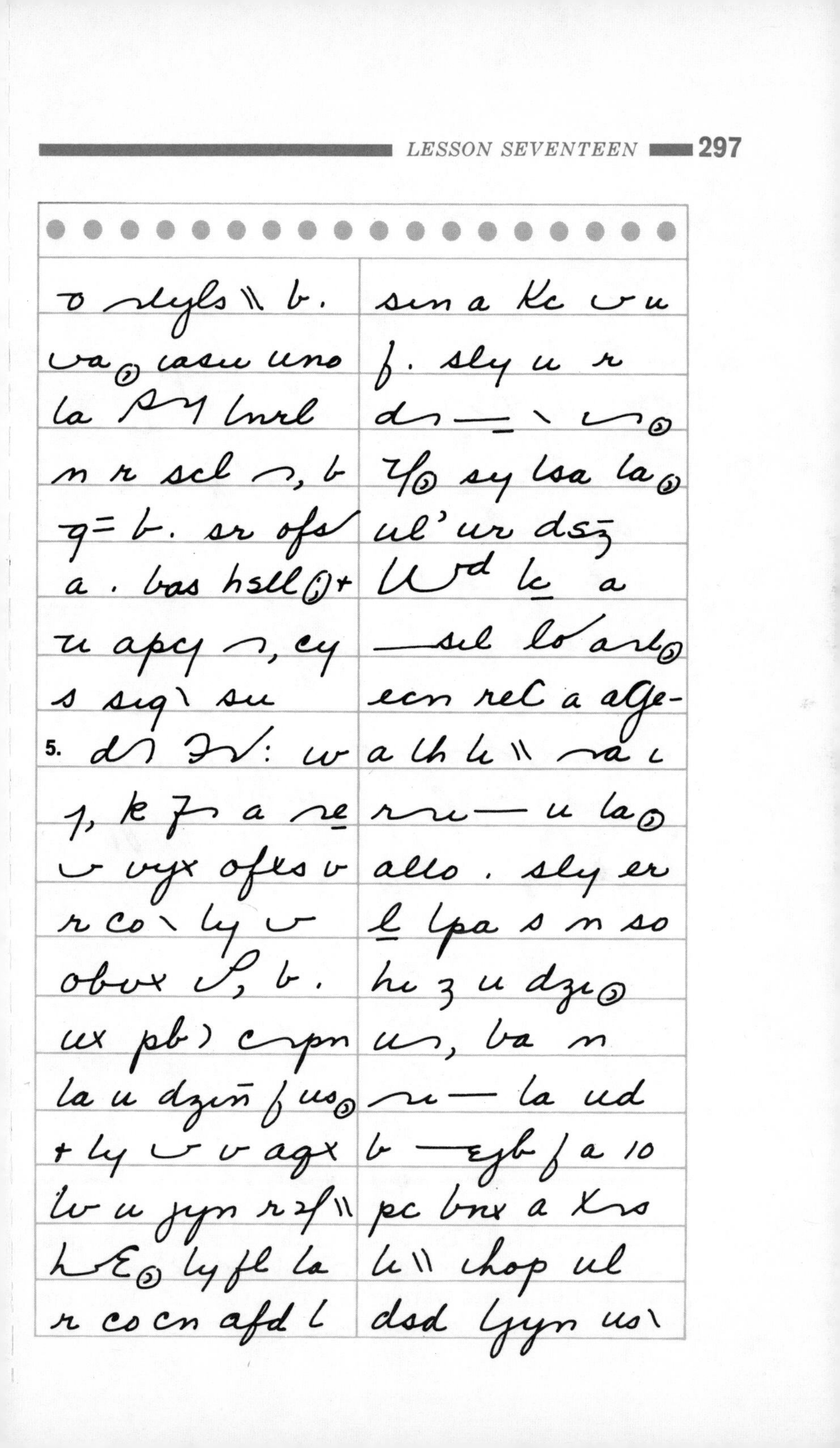

5.

6.

Key To Lesson 17

1. Dear Mrs. Wall: The object of this letter is to tell you about the tremendous inventory sale that we[2] are holding at our Elm Street warehouse on February 27. With the spring season so close at hand, we[4] are especially anxious

to make space for our new line; and we are, therefore, offering generous discounts on[6] our entire stock. (¶) This is no ordinary sale. The dresses you will see on display were purchased from world-famous[8] manufacturers of women's clothing, and they usually sell for considerably more than we are asking.[10] Whether you want a sport dress or a more formal outfit for evening wear, you will find it here. (¶) Why not take[12] a few minutes to come in and look around. Yours truly, *(130 words)*

2. Dear Mr. Banks: I have just seen the independent survey made by your committee on the poor quality to[2] be found in certain merchandise carried in various local stores. (¶) I think some of your charges are extremely[4] serious, and I strongly urge you to speak with your attorney before you do anything definite about[6] your idea to publish your findings. I feel sure that he will be inclined to agree that publication of this[8] report would probably result in legal action against you. (¶) Please let me know what you decide to do. Very[10] truly yours, *(102 words)*

3. Dear Sir: When I spoke with you on November 3, I made it quite plain that it was absolutely essential for[2] the material we ordered to be delivered no later than January 13. You said it would take[4] a period of approximately two months to make this particular shipment. (¶) It is now January[6] 6, and we are beginning to worry because we have received only partial shipment on this order. As I[8] told you, a delay of even a single day would result in a great financial loss to our firm; and we would[10] appreciate your doing whatever is necessary to speed this shipment along. (¶) We are sure you understand[12] that your ability to handle this initial order will determine our future relationship. Yours[14] truly, *(141 words)*

4. Dear Sir: This is in reply to your inquiry of August 4 in which you asked about the special courses open[2] to men who are stationed at the military hospital. (¶) In previous years, our university offered[4] a series of such courses; and

preliminary arrangements are now being made to do the same this year.[6] Although a complete summary of subjects is not yet ready, we are almost certain that we will repeat our[8] course in American history because it proved so popular last semester. Numerous men who took the[10] course made a definite point of letting us know how much they had enjoyed it. (¶) If you would like to spend some of your[12] spare time taking one of our splendid courses, you have only to fill out the application blank that is enclosed.[14] No specific requirements are necessary and no charge is made for books or materials. (¶) By the way, I[16] assume you know that permission to enroll in our school must be granted by the senior officer at the base[18] hospital; and your application must carry his signature. Sincerely yours, *(194 words)*

5. Dear Mr. Farmer: I have just come from a meeting with various officials of our company. They were obviously[2] impressed by the unusual publicity campaign that you designed for us, and they were very anxious[4] to have you join our staff. (¶) However, they feel that our company cannot afford to sign a contract with you[6] for the salary you are demanding. I am, therefore, sorry to say that, unless you are disposed toward taking[8] a slightly lower amount, we cannot reach an agreement at this time. (¶) May I remind you that, although the[10] salary we are willing to pay is not so high as you desire, you must bear in mind that you would be eligible[12] for a 10 percent bonus at Christmas time. (¶) I hope you will decide to join us. If you do, will you please call[14] me between 9:30 and 10:00 tomorrow morning. Cordially, *(151 words)*

6. Dear Mr. Hollis: Sales in this territory have been unusually high in recent months, and there has been a[2] continuous demand for the farm machinery that we manufacture. You, too, will find it financially[4] beneficial to carry our splendid line. (¶) A brief phone call to our main office will bring one of our agents to[6] visit you and explain the terms under which we will grant you the right to handle our equipment. Yours truly, *(79 words)*

Name............................Class.........Date................

Writing Assignment—Lesson 17

1. I thought you understood that it is usually customary to check the financial records before an initial order is sent on credit.

2. The officials of our hospital are desirous of thanking you for your gracious and generous help.

3. The speaker had nothing definite to say about the tremendous losses felt by various manufacturers in this territory.

4. Junior members of the American Library Club will receive a special bonus book by a world-famous author.

5. Thank you for the courteous answer to my inquiry concerning my spring supply of stationery.

6. We are sorry that you object to the manner in which we handled your previous order.

7. An inspection will probably show that the trouble with your machinery is not very serious.

8. We have had a continuous demand from numerous independent shop owners for additional display material.

Lesson 18

RULE 50 | **For the sounds of "nse" and "nsy" write a disjoined slant.**

You have learned that the final sounds of "er" and "ter' are represented by a slant that is joined to the letter or mark of punctuation that precedes it. In the present rule, however, you are instructed to write a disjoined slant – which simply means that it will not be joined to the letter or mark of punctuation that goes before it.

The word **assure,** as you know, is written aSu . If the sound of "nse" is added to this word to form *assurance,* you write a disjoined slant at the end of the outline: **assurance** aSu/ . In the same way, the word **rely** is rlu and you write **reliance** rlu/ .

Study these examples:

balance	bl/	**license**	ls/
announce	a-/	**allowance**	al-/
assistance	ass/	**since**	s/

insurance	nsu/	**correspondence**	Cs—/
convinced	kvT	**accordance**	aCd/
entrance	nT/	**expense**	xp/
remittance	rml/	**response**	rs/
convenience	kvn/	**financing**	fn/
confidence	kfd/	**experience**	xpy/
distance	ds/	**preference**	pf/

How will you form the plurals of these words? You will simply follow the rule for any outline that ends in a mark of punctuation and double the slant – as in **senses** s// ; **responses** rs// .

You write:

1. reference ________________ **2. expenses** ________________

3. attendance ________________ **4. conference** ________________

5. chance ________________ **6. evidence** ________________

7. difference ________________ **8. appearance** ________________

9. instances ________________ **10. defense** ________________

11. maintenance ________________ **12. influence** ________________

Confirmation:

1. rf/ 2. xp// 3. al—/ 4. kf/

5. C/ 6. evd/ 7. df/ 8. ape/

9. ns// 10. df/ 11. mtn/ 12. nfu/

This sound of "nse" may also occur in the middle of a word. When it does, you will follow the same rule and write a disjoined slant.

Study these examples:

responsible rs/b **principle** p/p

sponsored s/̄ **announcement** a-/-

You write:

1. expensive ______ **2. sincerely** ______

3. compensation ______ **4. responsibility** ______

Confirmation:

1. xp/v 2. s/el 3. kp/1 4. rs/b)

This rule also states that the disjoined slant will be used to represent the sound of "nsy"—the sound that is heard in *agency* or *fancy*. Thus: **agency** aj/ ; **fancy** f/ ; **emergency** emj/ ; **efficiency** efs/ .

Read these sentences:

1. s/ v h no rs/ l m L, il gv . akl l a rs/b aj/.

2. u v r asu/ la a al-/ lb rd y . bl/ s pd n ald/ v . 2rs a-/ a r kA/.

Key:

1. **Since I have had no response to my letter, I will give the account to a responsible agency.**

2. You have our assurance that an allowance will be made if the balance is paid in accordance with the terms announced at our conference.

RULE 51	Omit t after the sounds of "k, p, f, x"; omit pt after m.

This rule teaches you how to handle such words as *act, instruct,* and *district* – words in which the sound of "k" is followed by *t*. Therefore, in compliance with the rule, you omit the *t* from the outline.

Study these examples:

acts	acs	district	dSc
instruct	nSc	expect	xpc
inspected	nsc̄	factory	fcy
project	pjc	protect	plc
affect	afc	practical	pccl
neglected	ngc̄	practically	pccl
respect	rsc	conflict	kfc
connected	kc̄	exactly	xcl

You write:

1. products ________ 2. contact ________

3. fact ________ 4. effect ________

5. practice ________ 6. selected ________

7. exact ________ 8. conducting ________

Confirmation:

1. pdcs 2. klc 3. fc 4. efc
5. pcs 6. slc̄ 7. xc 8. kdc̲

Similarly, you are instructed to eliminate *t* after the sounds of "p, f," and "x."

Study these examples:

except	xp	**left**	lf
adopt	adp	**gift**	gf
accepting	xp̲	**next**	nx
acceptable	xpb	**text**	tx

You write:

1. accept ____________ 2. draft ____________

3. kept ____________ 4. swiftly ____________

5. context ____________ 6. pretext ____________

Confirmation:

1. xp 2. df 3. cp 4. swfl
5. klx 6. ptx

The second part of this rule instructs you in the handling of such words as *attempt* and *prompt*. Both the *p* and *t* are omitted and the outline ends with *m*.

Study these examples:

prompt	pm	**attempt**	atm
exempt	xm	**attempted**	atm̄

RULE 52 | **When the nature of an outline is such that the capitalization rule cannot be applied, write r for the medial sound of a vowel + "r."**

You know that **chat** is Cl and **shot** is Sl . You also know that when the sound of a vowel plus "r" occurs in the middle of a word, you capitalize the preceding letter. But what if the letter preceding these sounds is already capitalized – for example: *chart* or *short?* The present rule says that you will simply write r.

Study these examples:

shortly	Srll	**charter**	Cr/
sharp	Srp	**church**	CrC
short	Srl	**chart**	Crl
shortage	Srlj	**natural**	nCrl
shorthand	Srlh—	**naturally**	nCrl

In the same way, since you cannot apply the capitalization rule to such words as *standard* or *central*, you will write **standard** 2— rd and **central** s— rl .

Brief Forms

without	wo	**whom**	hm
collect	cc	**known**	no
sample	sam	**conclusion**	kclj

once, circumstance	c/	**individual, individually**	ndv
describe, description	des		

Abbreviations

post office	po	**memorandum**	memo
figure	fg	**inch**	in
page	p	**total**	tol
parcel post	pp		

Additional Words

described	des̄	**performance**	pfm/
describing	des_	**individuals**	ndvs
descriptive	desv	**samples**	sams
collection	ccj	**sampled**	sam̄
collected	cc̄	**pages**	ps
importance	ip/	**figures**	fgs
inches	ins	**figured**	fḡ

Reading Exercises

1. rd) —an: i	s/e F, op r di
s/el rGl. fc la	f f— —① ev
u S- dd n reC	rsē k bys lol O
u \\ n Cc r rCds①	h/a) del/ \ th
unl la. dfk	me n nl k
ocT cs edd nv	F dg a/\\ +
. Kc aD' l; fu\	ogs① b lso F
aT S- as nv b	ndv slgns hu
s- F r fcy b	obv+ rcgnz .
pp① + uc xpc	cp/v th Uhl
l l arc Srll \ ul	pjc\\ . gf u ga
2. drs Gdn: a.	n ny v u
Kcl v r di bz	sn l q a lq va
me f a nu	Ud hp l fn/
chns hsll① er	. xp/ v bld th
hpe l a/ la.	—s—d hsll\
rs/ l r apl z	u Sd fl v
vn g/ ln e h	pd v. ass/
hop \\ n.6 ros	uv gv \\ lq u

c/ aq f u ci hp
+ ksj \ s
3. -ds' rv=: n
u L v pn9o u
Ō 10 Yds v 18⊖
un fBc deō n r
cal o p 21 \\ hEo
u ngc̄ l ndca
. xc Sd v —bu
la u v-⊙+ elo
Yo n als Yfl
lh O ul uv klc̄
us ab. cl/ u
dzi \ ul
4. d) ps: uz v
—gd lrd.
reso u lf f
re o lh \ lgu
uds r x el pccl

+ Sd pv v suc\\
zu sf, o ul
als Lklc s
v. —m kc̄ v
. aj/ u —ī + l
se f T s ne
C/ v arf a kAl
f nx vk \ c
5. d) lq: . po
as f, a— | a Srp
nCs n. ras f
nSw/ o al pcps
la r s-b F,⊖
—c' ral \
nCrlo lh l afc
. pss gō f dl v
r pdcs \\ lgl
d b a q kon/ cf
a Crl v—d p

la d hpr —m
fq lh adjl Cq \
lu⊙ Y/⊙ ac o lh
sysy prl \ ul
6. dl —q': a
lrPy Srly v
pp/ rcs l cpsb
f us llv pl r
prs v dl b
ja 2 \ hE⊙ a
Ly S- s xpc̄ vn
. nx vk o 2⊙ +
il se la. lebcs
u ō r p= + s-
vo X dla \\ ln
v sy la lh
hpn̄⊙ b ln Su
ul lls— la e
i n no va

rs/b f. C|| la
cz lh Srly \ vlu
7. dl gsn : ln
ncz a l, v
nas l hn cd
lc u ls— sas
v r nu lu v
zyy \ z ss —my/
n lh dSc⊙ l
as b —u xpyl
la c/ lz sas
v b nsc̄ b pscv
Ks⊙ ls fr ez/ f
r ssm l kv/
ls l adp r lu\\
chop lh pcs res
v u aSol \ ul
8. j: C|| la r abs
by— u kvl

du n Sd re
(pa. bl/ o u
akl ul nx roo\\
c rlz. cp/ v cp
p v u pa--(;)
+ cno(,) lo(,) hv
aqx uv lcc.
mne la s ō
lu \ hE(,) chop
la u lq rCdv
ps pa-l nab
u lrc alv/ f
re n lh ns/\
ul

9. d) Fr-: vn
u slē r a// l
Kdc. pb) f u
pdc(,) u Sō
evd/ v rsc f
r (vc + r ab)
lh—l lh q
rs/b) \\ uv
u aSu/ la r
hl oq l du ls
ulro, l dZv u
kfd/ \ s

10. dK: ls a kn
pcs arq s
sfr// l xp Os
vo gv l Ks axc
dl da \ w Psnl
nov ns// n
vC Ks v b cp
va f 06 roo\\
ul b gd lno
la er a ro
rs/b oq \ la
s y e plc r

Key to Lesson 18

1. My dear Mr. Allen: I sincerely regret the fact that your shipment did not reach you. (¶) In checking our records, I note[2] that the difficulty occurred because we did not have the correct address listed for you. Another shipment[4] has now been sent from our factory by parcel post, and you can expect it to arrive shortly. Yours truly,[6] *(60 words)*

2. Dear Mrs. Gardner: At the conclusion of our drive to raise money for a new children's hospital, we are happy[2] to announce that the response to our appeal was even greater than we had hoped. (¶) In the six months since we first[4] opened our drive for funds, we have received contributions totaling over half a million dollars. This money not[6] only came from large agencies and organizations, but also from individual citizens who[8] obviously recognized the importance of this worthwhile project. (¶) The gift you gave in memory of your son will[10] go a long way toward helping to finance the expense of building this splendid hospital. You should feel very proud[12] of the assistance you have given. (¶) Thank you once again for your kind help and consideration. Sincerely, *(139 words)*

3. My dear Miss Rivers: In your letter of June 9, you ordered 10 yards of 18-inch fabric described in our[2] catalog on page 21. (¶) However, you neglected to indicate the exact shade of blue that you want; and[4] we will, therefore, not attempt to fill this order until you have contacted us about the color you desire.[6] Yours truly, *(62 words)*

4. Dear Mr. Price: I was very glad to read the memorandum you left for me on Thursday. I think your ideas[2] are extremely practical and should prove very successful. (¶) As you suggested, I will attempt to contact[4] some of the men connected with the agency you mentioned and will see if there is any chance of arranging[6] a conference for next week. Cordially, *(67 words)*

5. Dear Mr. Long: The post office has just announced a sharp increase in the rates for insurance on all packages[2] that are sent by first-class mail. Naturally, this will affect the prices quoted for delivery of our products[4]. (¶) I think it would be a great convenience if a chart were made up that would help our men figure this additional[6] charge. Will you, therefore, act on this suggestion promptly. Yours truly, *(71 words)*

6. Dear Mr. Glass: A temporary shortage of paper makes it impossible for us to live up to our promise[2] of delivery by January 2. However, a large shipment is expected within the next week[4] or two; and I will see that the textbooks you ordered are printed and sent without extra delay. (¶) I am very[6] sorry that this happened, but I am sure you will understand that we were in no way responsible for the[8] circumstances that caused this shortage. Very truly yours, *(89 words)*

7. Dear Mr. Grayson: I am enclosing a list of names to whom I would like you to send samples of our new line of[2] stationery. As sales manager in this district, it has been my experience that once these samples have been[4] inspected by prospective customers, it is far easier for our salesmen to convince them to adopt our[6] line. (¶) I

hope this practice meets with your approval. Yours truly, *(70 words)*

8. Gentlemen: Circumstances that are absolutely beyond my control do not permit me to pay the balance[2] on my account until next month. (¶) I realize the importance of keeping up with my payments; and I know, too,[4] how anxious you are to collect the money that is owed to you. However, I hope that my long record of prompt[6] payment will enable you to make allowance for me in this instance. Yours truly, *(75 words)*

9. Dear Mr. Freeman: When you selected our agency to conduct the publicity for your product, you showed[2] evidence of respect for our work and our ability to handle this great responsibility. (¶) You have my[4] assurance that our whole organization will do its utmost to deserve your confidence. Sincerely, *(58 words)*

10. Dear Customer: It is a common practice among some manufacturers to accept orders without giving[2] their customers an exact delivery date. I have personally known of instances in which customers[4] have been kept waiting for over six months. (¶) You will be glad to know that we are a more responsible organization.[6] That is why we protect our customers by giving them a written guarantee of delivery within[8] two weeks. Very truly yours, *(85 words)*

Writing Assignment – Lesson 18

1. In accordance with your memorandum, I have attempted to contact a company from whom we can charter a bus for the convenience of those individuals who attend our next conference.

2. You have my assurance that, once you have shown evidence of financial responsibility in the form of insurance, I will instruct our agency to issue your license.

3. It has been my experience that, except in unusual circumstances, compensation is paid promptly for the type of accident you describe.

4. I did not realize the importance of the announcement you made in the memorandum received by the district office.

5. In figuring my total balance, you neglected to make a correct allowance for the shortage that occurred.

6. Will you accept some free samples of our principal products?

7. This is the man without whom I could not have conducted such a successful campaign.

8. We ask your assistance in helping us collect the amount that is due.

Lesson 19

RULE 53 | **For the suffixes "ful and fully" and for the final sound of "fy," write** *f* **.**

Study these examples:

careful	*caf*	**respectfully**	*rscf*
useful	*usf*	**beautifully**	*btf*
***hopeful**	*hopf*	**notify**	*ntf*
wonderful	*w—rf*	**qualify**	*qlf*
carefully	*caf*	**justified**	*jsf*

*Note that the long vowel is retained in this word to avoid conflict with the outline for the word **helpful** *hpf*.

You write:

1. respectful ____________ **2. colorful** ____________

3. beautiful ____________ **4. colorfully** ____________

5. fearfully ____________ **6. specify** ____________

7. qualified ____________ **8. simplified** ____________

Confirmation:

1. rscf 2. cLf 3. blf 4. cLf
5. fef 6. ssf 7. glf 8. sspf

In Lesson 18 you learned that *t* is omitted after the sounds of "k, p, f," and "x." Thus, **fact** fc ; **gift** gf ; **next** nx .

The following rule is similar to this and deals with the dropping of *d* when it comes before certain sounds.

RULE 54 | **Omit d before "m" and "v."**

Study these examples:

admit	al	**advisory**	avzy
admittance	al/	**advised**	avz
admission	ay	**advisable**	avzb
admire	are	**advancement**	av/-
advise	avz	**advanced**	av/
advice	avs	**advances**	av//

RULE 55 | **For the sounds of "inter" and "enter," write a capital** N **.**

Study these examples:

enter n
interstate nsa
entertainment nln-
interrupt np
interested n,-
uninteresting un,

You write:

1. entered ____________ **2. entering** ____________

3. internal ____________ **4. interesting** ____________

5. interests ____________ **6. international** ____________

Confirmation:

1. n̄ 2. n 3. nnl 4. n,
5. n,, 6. nnjl

Notice that this rule refers specifically to the sounds of "inter" and "enter"–not to "intra, intri," or "intro." These latter sounds, you will recall, were incorporated into the rule dealing with the writing of capital *T* for medial "tr" in such words as **intrastate** nTsa ; **intricate** nTcl ; **introduce** nTds ; **introduction** nTdc/ .

You have learned to write a disjoined slant to represent the sounds of "nse" and "nsy" in such words as **insurance** nSu/ and **agency** aj/ . In the following rule, you will learn that s/ also represents a certain sound.

RULE 56 | For the sounds of "self" and "selves," write s/ .

Study these examples:

self	s/	**yourself**	us/
self-interest	s/n,	**itself**	ts/
myself	ms/	**himself**	hs/
herself	Hs/	**self-addressed**	s/aD,

You are also instructed to write s/ for the sound of "selves." In other words, it is not necessary to double the mark of punctuation to indicate the formation of a plural. Thus, **themselves** ts/ and **ourselves** rs/ . The only exception to this is the word **yourselves** which is written us// to avoid conflict with **yourself** us/ . In all other examples of this rule, there can be no confusion because words in this group exist only in the singular or plural form – never both. For example, ms/ can only be read as **myself** because there is no such word *myselves*. Similarly, you will know that rs/ is **ourselves** because there is no singular form for this word.

Brief Forms

move	mv	**auto**	A
perhaps	pps	**throughout**	Tuo
entitle	ntl		

Abbreviations

mile

railroad

railway

mortgage

associate

north

south

east

west

feet, foot

Additional Words

grateful

moving

moved

movement

removed

removal

removing

movers

northern

eastern

southern

western

automotive

automatic

automobile

automatically

entitled

entitles

associated

association

associations

railroads

mortgagee

miles

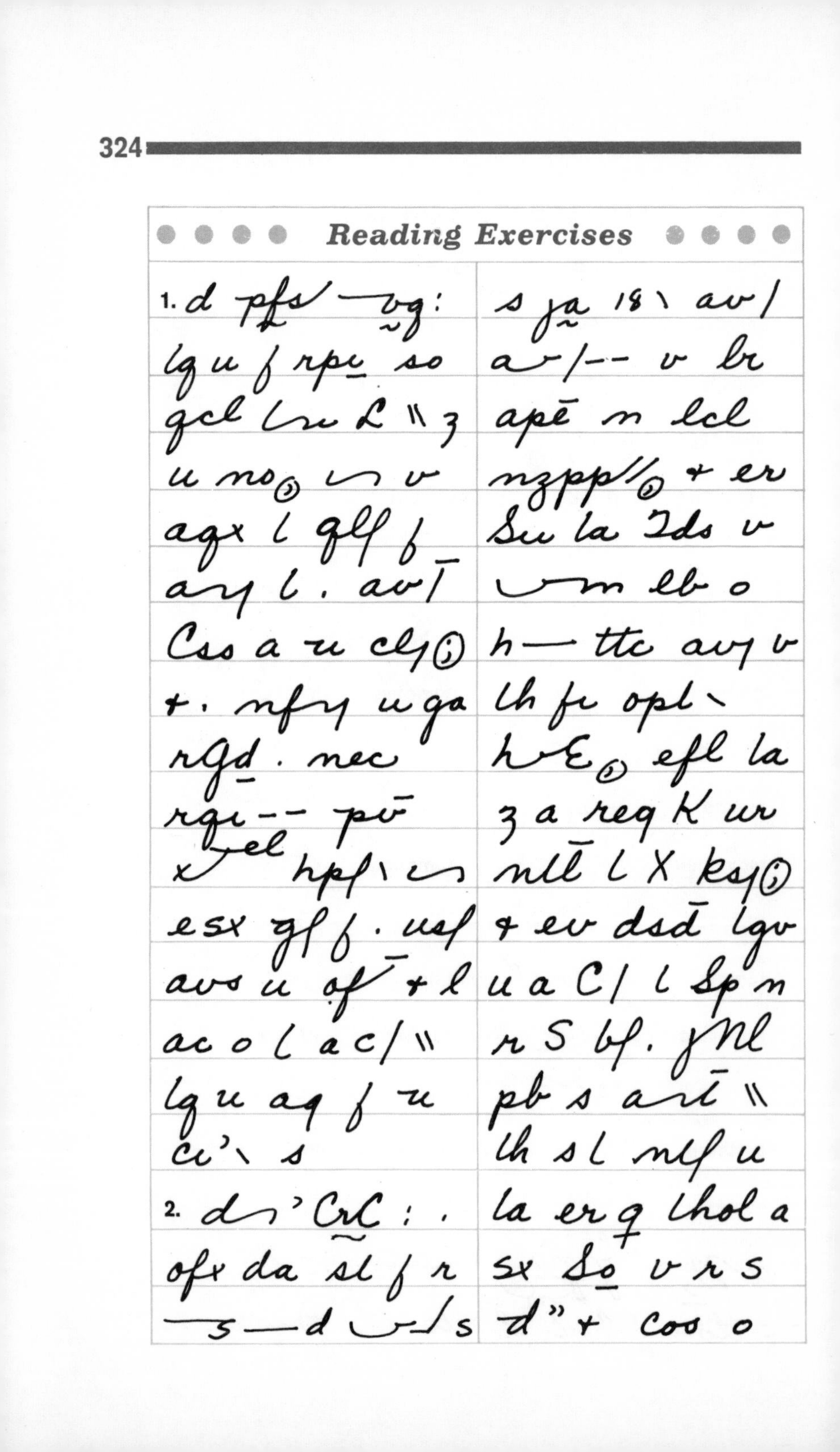

Reading Exercises

1.

2.

ja 17 Jr 6 l 9°\
u o l l rs/lk
n lse. — rf
Bgns la l b
avlb lu \ cu
3. rd hal:
n aCd/ u
nScps w
nsc u la,
cal caf + u
sy lsa la idu
n Sa u opn\
allo i arl la
. Oal apel s
qi cLf i
f— no,
v. lyl x el
uN,\ Jql
i do- fl l l

akps enf l
psf. q xpl
nolo n p
l lgT \ ilg
T la. ql)
v. pp s v
po + dz n k
pl. x 2 — rds
v. co la dd.
p= \\ h i b n
Cq v lh pjc
rsl id v
ns, la. jb
b dn aq +
id n v aGe
l xp l \ ill
4. ds: — pp
v koT lsl
la ly cn psb

afd a nu
Arbl \ v u
dn . sa lq?
v u lol rus/
la a nu cr s
lo xp/v ?? ym
20 n a r
Sor + ll
us xpn h r
hΘ pa- —pn
rcol ez lon
a blf nu crf .
rlvl ll me\
vl ur he(3)
lc r a .
v—rf nu
rdls la v
f, b dē Jr .
fcy \ se f

rus/h e v
Kbin caf
KScj v bu)
v li" ura
lso fl Je lsc
r rep f a
dmSj rd\
af nl a fu
rus(3) ul
lls— y Tsv
Arbl on// Tus
. d/v b sa
la lh cr s so
ez l h —l la
l lro dis
ls/\ uol
5. drs dS: pps
uv fgln la
pa-o u bl

Sd v reC uso
ap 19\ sa e
sc la u s— us
u Cc n. s/aD,
env la s ncz\
ul

6. dl dvs: ud
lc ttc a so-
ttl u h- sC
w njy u
assoj v u Luo
.ys\ w l-
ks us/ fCnl
lw Uc. so
—csl v u.
+ i Lul rgl
la uw dsd
Lw u ofss
laT s)\ . rep

v h ul b
dl n u nu
lcj as lr xP,
s dzi lb z
hpl z psb. +
v Sln la h
l du vlE h
c lb usf lu
n E va \ s

7. ds: v sy
la udd n
aPv v. sld
b vC e s-u
l, D\ e lo e
v Sv u b,
n,, vn e sd
S- b ry xP.
+ e rgl la
lh z n vl u

v= \\ l avyd
ne sC E/ n.
fC l u caf
ssf u pf/ n
rGd l. m
n C S- s
lb d \ ul
8. d/ bc: w
lc a s p))
n C u a
b N; z a psb
s f u nu
p- \ / v l
p)) s ab 5
s N v. s)
+. T ls a
Srl ds/ l. U\
bo r lcā n
a H fl v. m

hu a + n a
fu s v.
rr \\ c Us—
la. k) T, co
hols. lq o
Ch l— + s/,
la u Klc L
f F nf/ \\
a L flos gv
dlL dess v
. p)) \ ul
9. /: Ch s lnlf
u la w ro-l
w F 59 S
ql) rd l 130
E s sl \\
lu p G u
rCds l ndca
u nu aD'

so la ic b Su
Z lb no Npj
n. dl v ru
sub l ru
rol raq \
ul

Key To Lesson 19

1. Dear Professor Blank: Thank you for replying so quickly to my letter. (¶) As you know, I am very anxious to[2] qualify for admission to the advanced courses at your college; and the information you gave regarding[4] the necessary requirements proved extremely helpful. I am especially grateful for the useful advice[6] you offered and will act on it at once. (¶) Thank you again for your kindness. Sincerely, *(75 words)*

2. Dear Miss Church: The official date set for our splendid winter sale is January 18. Advance announcements[2] have already appeared in local newspapers, and we are sure that thousands of women will be on hand to take[4] advantage of this fine opportunity. However, we feel that as a regular customer you are[6] entitled to extra consideration; and we have decided to give you a chance to shop in our store before[8] the general public is admitted. (¶) This is to notify you that we are going to hold a special showing[10] of our sale dresses and coats on January 17 from six to nine o'clock. You owe it to yourself[12] to come in to see the wonderful bargains that will be available to you. Cordially yours, *(137 words)*

3. My dear Mr. Hall: In accordance with your instructions, I have inspected your latest catalog carefully;[2] and I am sorry to say that I do not share your opinion. Although I admit that the overall appearance[4] is quite colorful, I found most of the material extremely uninteresting. Frankly, I don't feel[6] it will accomplish enough to justify the great expense involved in putting it together. I think further[8] that the quality of the paper is very poor and does not come up to the usual standards of the company[10] that did the printing. (¶) Had I been in charge of this project myself, I would have insisted that the job be done[12] again; and I would not have agreed to accept it. Yours truly, *(131 words)*

4. Dear Sir: Many people have convinced themselves that they cannot possibly afford a new automobile. Have you[2]

done the same thing? Have you told yourself that a new car is too expensive? (¶) Why not stop in at our showroom and let us explain[4] how our time-payment plan makes it easy to own a beautiful new car for relatively little[6] money. While you are here, look around at the wonderful new models that have just been delivered from the[8] factory. See for yourself how we have combined careful construction with beauty of line. (¶) You may also feel free to[10] ask our representative for a demonstration ride. After only a few miles, you will understand why millions[12] of automobile owners throughout the country have been saying that this car is so easy to handle that[14] it almost drives itself. Yours very truly, *(148 words)*

5. Dear Mrs. Dash: Perhaps you have forgotten that payment on your bill should have reached us on April 19. (¶) May we[2] ask that you send us your check in the self-addressed envelope that is enclosed. Yours truly, *(35 words)*

6. Dear Mr. Davis: I would like to take a moment to tell you how much I have enjoyed my association[2] with you throughout the years. I have always considered myself fortunate to have worked so closely with you, and I truly[4] regret that you have decided to move your offices to another city. (¶) The representative[6] with whom you will be dealing in your new location has already expressed his desire to be as helpful as[8] possible, and I am certain that he will do whatever he can to be useful to you in every way.[10] Sincerely, *(103 words)*

7. Dear Sir: I am sorry that you did not approve of the method by which we sent your last order. We thought we were[2] serving your best interests when we made shipment by railway express, and we regret that this was not what you wanted.[4] (¶) To avoid any such error in the future, will you carefully specify your preference in regard[6] to the manner in which shipment is to be made. Yours truly, *(70 words)*

8. Dear Mr. Bright: I have looked at some properties in which you may be interested as a possible site for[2] your

new plant. One of these properties is about five miles north of the city and the other lies a short distance[4] to the west. Both are located within a hundred feet of the main highway and within a few miles of the railroad.[6] (¶) I understand that the County Trust Company holds the mortgage on this land and suggest that you contact them[8] for further information. (¶) A letter follows giving detailed descriptions of the properties. Yours truly, *(97 words)*

9. Gentlemen: This is to notify you that I have recently moved from 59 South Quality Road to[2] 130 East Center Street. (¶) Will you please change your records to indicate my new address so that I can be[4] sure there will be no interruption in the delivery of my subscription to your monthly magazine. Yours[6] truly, *(61 words)*

Name..............................*Class*.........*Date*.......... ....

Writing Assignment – Lesson 19

1. Membership in our automobile association will entitle you to a subscription to our interesting and useful magazine.

---

2. I respectfully request that you give me a chance to justify your confidence in me.

---

3. Our President accepted a position with an international firm on the West Coast and he will be moving there shortly.

---

4. I strongly advise that you carefully discuss the internal organization of the company among yourselves and notify me of your decision.

---

5. If you will forward your request in the self-addressed envelope that is enclosed, we will send you a colorful folder that describes our beautiful new automatic washer.

6. We would like to be helpful in this instance, but although we greatly admire the man you mentioned, we do not consider ourselves qualified to offer advice on his plan.

7. Railroads throughout the country have announced a reduction of fares for all interstate travel.

Lesson 20

Let's examine some words in which two vowels occur together but have only one sound. For example, *lease, tail, built*. In these words, the sound of only one vowel is heard. However, there are some words in which two vowels occur together – both of which are pronounced: *actual, fuel, graduate, ruin*. It is to this latter group of vowel sounds that this next rule applies.

RULE 57 | **When a word contains two medial pronounced consecutive vowels, the first vowel sound is written.**

Study these examples:

annual		**actual**	
mutual		**dual**	
fuel		**ruin**	

gradual	*gdul*	**trial**	*tl*
poet	*pol*	**manual**	*mul*
diameter	*ds/*	**diet**	*dil*

When an outline ends in a vowel, write the final vowel omitting any vowel sound that precedes it: **graduate** *gda* ; **create** *ca* ; **radio** *rdo* ; **area** *aa* .

Here is a summary of the various rules concerned with the writing and/or omission of vowels.

1. Write all initial and final vowels: **edge** *ej* ; **data** *dla* ; **value** *vlu* ; **item** *is* .
2. Omit all medial short vowels: **sell** *sl* ; **check** *Cc* .
3. Omit long vowels in words of more than one syllable unless covered by a specific rule: **music** *mzc* ; **prevail** *pvl* .
4. When "ing" or "ed" are added to a root word that contains a long vowel, retain vowel: **sailing** *sal* ; **reached** *rec* .
5. When the root word outline ends in a vowel, retain vowel when suffix is added: **reliable** *rlib* ; **lightly** *lil* ; **happiest** *hpe,* ; **evaluation** *evluj* ; **myself** *ms/* ; **fairness** *fa?* ; **compliance** *kpi/* ; **gaiety** *ga)* .
6. When a long vowel is followed by a sound that is represented by a mark of punctuation, retain this long

vowel in outline: **variety** ; **science** ; **client** ; **remind** ; **acquaint** .

7. When a word contains two pronounced consecutive vowels, one long and one short, the first vowel is written: **ruin** ; **gradual** ; **poet** .

8. When an outline ends in a vowel, write the final vowel and omit any vowel that precedes it: **graduate** ; **create** .

There is one sound in our language that has no alphabetic representation – the sound of "zh" heard in *visual, casual, treasure.* It is to this sound that the following rule applies.

RULE 58 | For the sound of "zh," write .

Study these examples:

casual		**visual**	
casualty		**treasury**	
pleasurable		**treasurer**	
leisurely		**measuring**	

You write:

1. pleasure ______ **2. enclosure** ______

3. treasure ______ **4. seizure** ______

5. enclosures ______ **6. measured** ______

7. measures ______ **8. treasured** ______

Confirmation:

1. -pz/ 2. ncz/ 3. Tz/ 4. sz/
5. ncz// 6. -nz/ 7. -nz// 8. Tz/

RULE 59 | For the sound of "sub," write s .

Study these examples:

submitted	sm̄	subsequently	ssq-l
substantial	ssx	substitute	sslu
subsistence	sss/	subtract	sTc

You write:

1. submit ______________ 2. substantially ______________

3. subsequent ______________ 4. substitution ______________

5. subway ______________ 6. submitting ______________

Confirmation:

1. sml 2. ssx 3. ssq- 4. ssl/
5. swa 6. sml

And now for the final rule in *Speedwriting* Shorthand.

RULE 60 | **For the sound of "trans," write T .**

Study these examples:

transaction	Tac/	**transferred**	Tf-
transmission	Tm/	**transportation**	Tsp/
transcription	Tcp/	**transit**	Tt

You write:

1. **transcript** ______________ 2. **transfer** ______________

3. **transferring** ______________ 4. **transport** ______________

Confirmation:

1. Tcp 2. Tf 3. Tf- 4. Tsp

Brief Forms

declare dec **pull** pu **pupil** pup

Abbreviations

miscellaneous	msc	**bureau**	Bu
pound	lb	**corporation**	corp
superintendent	supt	**square**	sq

administrate, administration ad

Additional Words

administrator	ad/	declared	dec̄
administrative	adv	declaration	dec/
administrators	ad//	superintendents	supls
pupils	pups	pounds	lbs

Reading Exercises

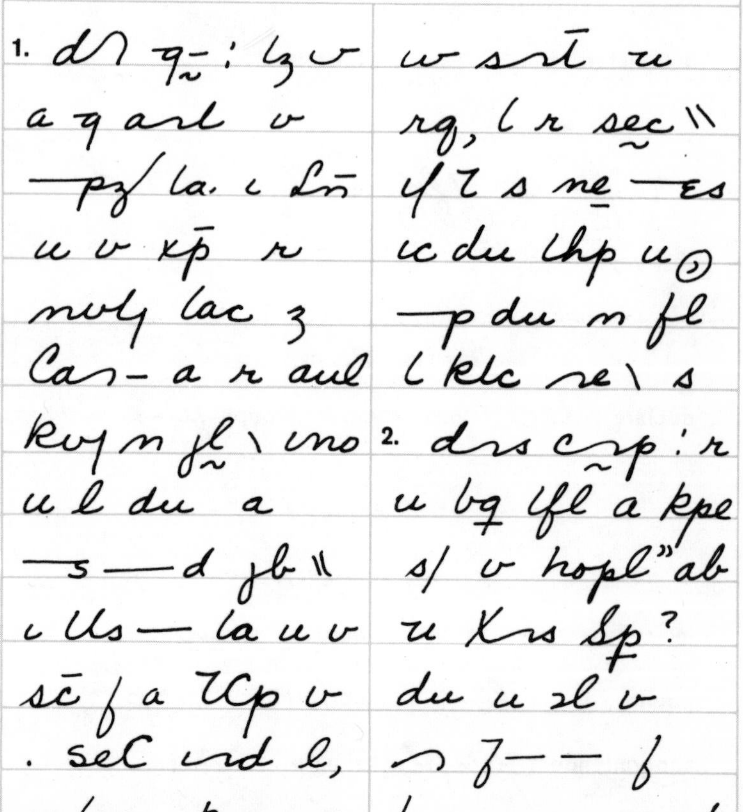

fr— . pp/
gf?? ɥ lhs .
cas⊙ ln ı rk—
la u 20 a r S
l nsc . fl fd
+ ıst Cz la e
cy \ lh le asb
gn n pop) Tu
. ys⊙ + nel o
u Xrs l, l
lk a 10 o 20
lb Tz/C, sd
p v r dlx

pdcs \\ er vn
ez vc ds/ v
al bs + s-a
Tsy⊙ + r dos
rm opE vd
+ sl vn ul

10° \ y n k n
+ p a e— l u
Sp plrs \ ul
3. ds' sra: .
Bu v Nnl afas
as a-/ . pq
v a —ypcC/la
u r fe hplf
us n u a-s
gvl —c" \ lh
Srl fls l gv
u pups a
—ce/ cd v .

— acv)) v .
Bu + l hp l
dv a g/N, n.
ads v gvl
ajll v lh lep))
uc obln lh

fls b srp D
u rg, l. ofs
v. supl v
scls n u aa\
cu

4. d Zq: . alC
Crl l gv u
vzul evd/ v.
fcs cga u kSn
. xcs cSu b r
corp du . p,
18 ys\ z uc se⊙
Z z nl a gdul
rz n. aul
dvd— — pd
br xchol// n.
F, 10 ys⊙ b n.
pyd s/ ln⊙ r
xc as db n

vlu v a ssg-
nCs n. sz v.
dvd— — dec \\
zfr z . fC s
kSn⊙ er nvlv
n usc Zacys
la l ca vn
ro ssx pfls f
us \ f lh rzn⊙
cdu n hzla l
avz u lb r x
z a saf nos-f
u sv \ us

5. rds: lh s n
rs/ l. L e rse
Fs u n vC
u rd ngy
rGd r Cgs f
lprv r-ls \\

ecn go a
2 — rd ra a
lh lu cs ⌒ fc//
r kō n dT m
, aCul c, \ f
x p. e nd l
no h ⌒
Sns ul ⌒.
. lgl v lu
nvlō. + ⌒
u rgi mul
⌒ elc c
lprl// \ ful
spi lh nfy
o. ncz Cd.
el b hpe lgo
u a xc ps f
r r-l Sos \
ul

6. d⌒ ⌒: w
p, h a lq
kV ⌒ . P
+ Vz v r co
ab . rGlb sul
n ⌒C e n⌒
fr rs/ \ z u
no. ev b lz
a q ⌒ v r
⌒pyes l vyx
cos n. s) la
of lBl aul
nCss n sly.
frs v hll
nSul/. X vey
bnxs. + T
fnx bnfs \\ ls
obvx la s ⌒,
b dn ida \ f

lh rzn⊙ ⌒ cl
a sx re v .
Bd v D" f Fr⊙
ap 5⊙ a 3^15 \\
n . mlu⊙ d
u rvu . l, v
usc sjsjs
la r ncz so
la u ra gv
re u opn
vn e re \
ul

7. rd) ve:
r F s ag+ lo
u Uf u bsl
us⊙ + er n
lo prd l
arl l \ eno
ec sal u E

nd + la dl
v us l b l
r Kul avy \\
vo- u s — us
a Tel O so la
e ra pv
rs/ \ ul

8. f: o ag 14 ,
O a q' lb
lp l rpl . l ,
h bcn \ l arv
ySd⊙ b ,
f — la l dd
n fl pl \\
vlz n la ,
rd a E/ vn
, rz .
dv v. lb⊙
+ vs re lsc

~ s_ c b	
dn\ id dpl	
ap ne sjs/	
uc nc la l	
sv ne .	
adjl xp/ v	
O a nu/\	
s	

Key to Lesson 20

1. Dear Mr. Grant: It was with a great amount of pleasure that I learned you have accepted our invitation to[2] act as chairman at our annual convention in July. I know you will do a splendid job. (¶) I understand[4] that you have asked for a transcript of the speech I made last year to open the convention, and I have submitted[6] your request to our Secretary. (¶) If there is anything else I can do to help you, please do not fail to contact[8] me. Sincerely, *(83 words)*

2. Dear Mrs. Camp: Are you beginning to feel a complete sense of hopelessness about your Christmas shopping? Do you[2] still have many friends for whom you have not yet found the proper gift? (¶) If this is the case, then I recommend that you[4] stop at our store to inspect the fancy food and imported cheese that we carry. This line has been gaining in[6] popularity through the years, and anyone on your Christmas list will welcome a one- or two-pound treasure chest made[8] up of our delicious products. (¶) We are within easy walking distance of all bus and subway transportation,[10] and our doors remain open every Wednesday and Saturday evening until ten o'clock. Why not come in and[12] put an end to your shopping problems. Yours truly, *(128 words)*

3. Dear Miss Small: The Bureau of Internal Affairs has announced the preparation of a motion picture that you[2] might find helpful for use in your American Government classes. This short film will give your pupils a clearer[4] idea of the many activities of the Bureau and will help to develop a greater interest[6] in the administration of government agencies of this type. (¶) You can obtain this film by simply directing[8] your request to the Office of the Superintendent of Schools in your area. Cordially yours, *(98 words)*

4. Dear Frank: The attached chart will give you visual evidence of the facts I gave you concerning the stocks issued[2]

by our corporation during the past 18 years. As you can see, there was only a gradual rise in the[4] annual dividends paid to our stockholders in the first 10 years; but in the period since then, our[6] stock has doubled in value with a subsequent increase in the size of the dividends declared. (¶) As far as the[8] future is concerned, we are involved in miscellaneous transactions that will create even more substantial[10] profits for us. For this reason, I do not hesitate to advise you to buy our stock as a safe investment[12] for your savings. Yours sincerely, *(125 words)*

5. My dear Sir: This is in response to the letter we received from you in which you made inquiry regarding our[2] charges for typewriter rentals. (¶) We cannot quote a standard rate at this time because many factors are considered[4] in determining the actual cost. For example, we need to know how many machines you will want, the[6] length of time involved, and whether you require manual or electric typewriters. (¶) If you will supply this[8] information on the enclosed card, we will be happy to give you an exact price for our rental service. Yours truly,[10] *(100 words)*

6. Dear Mr. March: I have just had a long conversation with the President and Treasurer of our company[2] about the regrettable situation in which we now find ourselves. As you know, we have been losing a great[4] many of our employees to various companies in the city that offer liberal annual[6] increases in salary, forms of health insurance, extra vacation bonuses, and other financial benefits.[8] (¶) It is obvious that something must be done immediately. For this reason, I am calling a special[10] meeting of the Board of Directors for Friday, April 5, at 3:15. (¶) In the meantime, would you review the[12] list of miscellaneous suggestions that are enclosed so that you may give me your opinion when we meet. Yours[14] truly, *(141 words)*

7. My dear Mr. White: Our firm is anxious to have you transfer your business to us, and we are not too proud to admit[2] it. We know we can satisfy your every need and that

dealing with us will be to our mutual[4] advantage. (¶) Won't you send us a trial order so that we may prove ourselves. Yours truly, *(55 words)*

8. Gentlemen: On August 14 I ordered a glass table top to replace the one I had broken. It arrived[2] yesterday, but I found that it did not fit properly. (¶) I realize now that I made an error when I measured[4] the diameter of the table, and I am writing to ask whether something can be done. I would deeply[6] appreciate any suggestion you can make that will save me the additional expense of ordering a[8] new one. Sincerely, *(83 words)*

—NOTICE—

You should soon receive your validated Speedwriting International Registration Form directly from New York.

If you do not receive it within one month, please contact:

THE SPEEDWRITING COMPANY
55 West 42 Street, New York, N.Y. 10036

Unless you possess this Form, you will lose all lifetime Employment, Transfer, and Brush-up privileges.

Writing Assignment – Lesson 20

1. All those who are graduating this fall should submit applications for the administrative positions open in our company.

2. The annual casualty rate has increased substantially in the past five years, and a variety of safety measures have been proposed by our bureau.

3. All transportation charges will be paid if salesmen submit expense accounts to the office of the treasurer.

4. We are confident that we can create a substantial demand for our product by sending out trial samples of merchandise.

5. Speak to the superintendent in regard to the actual amount of fuel used in the building during the winter months.

6. It is a pleasure to send you a special two-pound gift selection of our famous cheese.

7. This transaction will serve a dual purpose. It will create a great many jobs at the plant and will result in more efficient production.

BRIEF FORM and STANDARD ABBREVIATION REVIEW

Lessons 16 through 20

1. Dear Miss Rose: Several years ago an independent group of men and women, who were particularly[2] interested in the field of education, decided to organize an association of junior and[4] senior high school teachers. (¶) These individuals thought that an organization of this kind would give teachers[6] throughout America a chance to meet and learn of new methods being developed to improve the level of[8] education as a whole. The idea met with immediate success, and the organization grew from an[10] initial membership of 55 to its present total of almost three thousand. (¶) The object of this[12] letter is to tell you that the southeast division of the American Association will hold its annual[14] meeting at the conclusion of the winter term. The date will probably be during the week of January[16] 18, but more definite information will be sent as soon as available. Sincerely yours, *(178 words)*

2. Dear Sir: The superintendent of our warehouse on West Elm Street has informed me that the volume of orders being[2] shipped has increased by approximately 20 percent during the past six months. (¶) In view of these circumstances,[4] I feel we should now consider moving to larger quarters. Therefore, we are looking for a building on the[6] north side of town that will provide us with at least an additional 5,000 square feet of space and with a[8] location no more than a mile or two from the railroad. Very truly yours, *(92 words)*

3. My dear Sir: This will acknowledge receipt of your letter of June 9. (¶) I have known the young man about whom you speak[2] for a number of years. He was once a pupil at our school and was described by his teachers as being unusually[4] intelligent and hard working. I recall that his health was always rather poor, but he was able[6] to hold miscellaneous jobs around town during his summer vacations. When I last saw him, he declared his[8] intention of

applying for a job with the parcel post division of the post office; and I understand[10] that his application was approved. Sincerely yours, *(109 words)*

4. Dear Mr. West: Our organization has set up a research bureau that will collect statistics and figures[2] regarding sales in and around our city. Such information will be of particular interest to[4] manufacturers in this area and will be furnished free of charge. (¶) The signature of your corporation's[6] president on the enclosed card will entitle you to a 12-page descriptive booklet that will give you additional[8] information about this unusual service. Sincerely yours, *(92 words)*

5. Dear Mr. Long: We are sending you 3 nine-ounce samples of our latest product as well as a one-pound box of[2] various cheese we manufacture. (¶) I have also written a memorandum to my secretary to[4] remind her that you are to receive a pair of tickets to our annual food show in September. Yours truly,[6] *(60 words)*

6. Dear Mr. Mark: Our company has decided to build a railway to connect our plant with the main track of the[2] Northwest Railroad. Doing so will enable us to transport our automobiles quickly and efficiently and[4] will help to speed up delivery to all parts of the country. (¶) I understand that you hold the mortgage on the[6] property we have in mind, and I would like to meet with you to discuss the sale of this land. Yours truly, *(78 words)*

–REVIEW–

Lessons 16 through 20

1. Dear Miss Blank: A mutual friend has submitted your name as one who might be interested in a chance to make[2] some extra money in your spare time. (¶) You can do so by selling our beautiful line of Christmas cards and gift

wrappings.[4] We not only pay a liberal amount for each box sold, but we also give a generous bonus to[6] the person in each city who sends us the largest order. (¶) If you feel inclined to accept our offer, you can[8] contact us by phoning the number shown above. We hope to hear from you. Yours truly, *(95 words)*

2. My dear Mr. Able: You are undoubtedly aware of the fact that we will shortly attempt to set up a[2] training program in our factory. The main purpose of this program is to instruct our employees in the proper[4] maintenance of our machinery. We are hopeful that it will also prove useful in helping our men[6] understand the importance of adopting the safety measures you advised in your annual report. (¶) In this[8] connection, I wonder if you could spare the time to speak at one of our sessions. I think you, more than anyone else,[10] could be helpful in getting this point across to the men. (¶) May I hear from you soon? Sincerely yours, *(117 words)*

3. My dear Mrs. Ash: I am very sorry that I could not speak with you myself when you called[2] yesterday. As my secretary told you, I was attending an extremely important conference at the time and was unable[4] to interrupt the meeting to answer the phone. (¶) I did, however, receive the message you left for me[6] and will arrange to transfer your account to our central branch as soon as you notify me of your correct address. (¶)[8] If there is any other way in which I can be of help, please do not hesitate to contact me. Cordially,[10] *(100 words)*

BRIEF FORMS AND STANDARD ABBREVIATIONS
— BOOK THREE —

about	ab	as	z
above	bv	ask	sc
absolute, ly	abs	associate	asso
acknowledge	ak	at	a
administrate	ad⌒	auto	A
administration	ad⌒	avenue	ave
advantage	avj	average	av
advertise	adv	be	b
again, st	ag	because	cs
almost	lmo	been	b
already	lr	began	bg
also	lso	begin	bg
always	lv	benefit	bnf
am	⌒	between	bl
America, n	a⌒	billion	B
amount	a⌒l	both	bo
an	a	boulevard	blvd
and	&	bureau	Bu
appreciate	ap	business	bs
approximate, ly	apx	busy	bz
are	r	but	b
around	r⌣	buy	b

by	b
call	cl
came	k
can	c
capital	cap
catalog	cat
cents	c
certificate	cert
certify	cert
charge	Cg
child	ch
children	chn
Christmas	Xs
circumstance	c/
collect	cc
come	k
committee	k
company	co
conclusion	kclj
consider	ks
continue	ku
contract	Kc
corporation	corp
correct	Kc
country	c/
credit	cr
customer	K
day	d
deal	dl
declare	dec
definite, ly	dfn
deliver	dl
delivery	dl
department	dpt
describe	des
description	des
develop	dv
difficult	dfk
difficulty	dfk
direct	D
discount	dis
doctor	dr
dollar, s	d
during	du
East	E
easy	ez

entitle	ntl	future	fc
envelope	env	given	gv
establish	esl	go	g
even	vn	good	g
evening	vn̲	government	gvt
ever	E	great	g̅
every	E	had	h
extra	X	has	as
extraordinary	Xo	have	v
fail	fl	he	h
federal	fed	held	hl
feel	fl	help	hp
feet	ft	him	h
field	fld	his	s
figure	fg	hole	hl
find	fi	hour	r
fine	fi	hundred	H
fire	fr	idea	id
firm	F	immediate, ly	ida
foot	ft	important	ip
for	f	in	n
full	fu	inch	in
fully	fu	independent	ind

individual, ly

initial, ly

intelligence

intelligent, ly

invoice

is

it

junior

keep

kind

known

letter

life

like

line

little

magazine

man

manufacture

many

maximum

member

memorandum

merchandise

mile

million

minimum

month

minute

miscellaneous

mortgage

move

necessarily

necessary

North

not

note

number

object

of

on

once

only

open

opinion

opportunity

order	O	prove	pv
organization	og	public	pb
organize	og	publish	pb
other	T	pull	pu
ounce	oz	pupil	pup
our	r	purchase	pC
out	ou	put	p
over	O	question	q
page	p	railroad	rr
pair	pr	railway	ry
parcel post	pp	real, ly	rl
particular, ly	P	regular, ly	reg
percent	pc	regulation	reg
perhaps	pps	represent	rep
place	pl	representative	rep
please	-p	result	rsl
poor	po	room	r
popular	pop	sale	s
post office	po	sample	sa
pound	lb	satisfaction	sal
president	P	satisfactory	sal
price	ps	satisfy	sal
probable, ly	pb	save	sv

school	scl	the	.
second	sec	their	T
secretary	sec	there	T
senior	sr	they	ty
several	sv	this	th
shall	S	those	tos
she	S	thought	to
ship	S	thousand	Td
signature	sig	throughout	Tuo
situation	sit	to	t
small	sma	too	to
South	S	total	tol
square	sq	under	U
stop	2o	until	ul
street	st	up	p
subject	sj	upon	pn
subscribe	sub	usual, ly	x
subscription	sub	very	v
success	suc	vice-president	VP
successful, ly	suc	volume	vol
superintendent	supt	warehouse	whs
telephone	tel	was	z
that	ta	we	e

week	wk	will	l
well	l	with	w
were	w	without	wo
West	W	woman	wm-
where	wr	world	Wo
while	wl	would	d
whole	hl	year	y
whom	hm	your	u
why	y		

NOW SUCCESS IS AT YOUR FINGERTIPS!

Very quickly you will have achieved your goal – a wonderfully satisfying career as a secretary. You have completed all of the theory of *Speedwriting* shorthand and have learned all the principles which make up this very efficient system. You have not only become familiar with the rules but you have had concentrated practice in writing the 3,000 words of highest frequency, which represent approximately 90 percent of everyday English. These words will form the basic framework of the dictation you will be taking on the job.

Now with confidence and enthusiasm you can move on to the final phase of your shorthand training – building speed and the automatization of an ever-increasing vocabulary. You will accomplish this

by taking two types of live dictation after you have successfully passed your Final Theory Test.

The first of these methods is called *repetitive dictation* or *speed building.* As a part of this program, you will be assigned a lesson from the dictation book as homework each day. You will write each of the letters several times in *Speedwriting* shorthand; and you will, of course, check your *Speedwriting* Dictionary for any word which is unfamiliar to you. When you return to class the following day, these letters will be dictated again and again at higher and higher speeds. This repetitive process serves the purpose of making the words a part of your working vocabulary and will help you to develop a greater and more varied automatic response.

The second type of dictation to which you will be introduced is known as *unfamiliar dictation.* You will learn to take dictation from material that you have not heard before – just as you will shortly be doing from your employer. In this class, too, you will take dictation tests at various speed levels and, having passed the last of them, you will be completely confident in your ability to take dictation accurately and quickly from any employer.

Refining your dictation skill is only part of your training though. You will also learn to transcribe your notes with accuracy and speed, and you will learn to turn out a letter which is a credit to you and the company you will represent. You will master this skill too in the final stage of your dictation course.

Your *Speedwriting* shorthand course has been planned with one objective – to enable you adequately to fulfill every office dictation requirement. If you apply yourself diligently and intelligently, you will be assured of future success when you go out into the business world.

LETTER PLACEMENT CHART

The placement of a letter on a page depends upon the length of the letter. For proper balance, both the margins and the position of the inside address must be varied for letters of different lengths. Eventually, a glance at your notes will enable you to judge the placement of your letter, but this requires a good deal of practice and experience. For the present, make use of the procedure given below as a guide to proper placement. Type date 14 line spaces from top of page.

WORDS	LENGTH OF LINE	LINES FROM DATE TO INSIDE ADDRESS
50	4 inches	10
75	4 inches	9
100	4 inches	8
125	5 inches	7
150	5 inches	6
175	5 inches	5
200	6 inches	4
225	6 inches	3
250	6 inches	2
300	6 inches	2

ENVELOPES, ADDRESSING

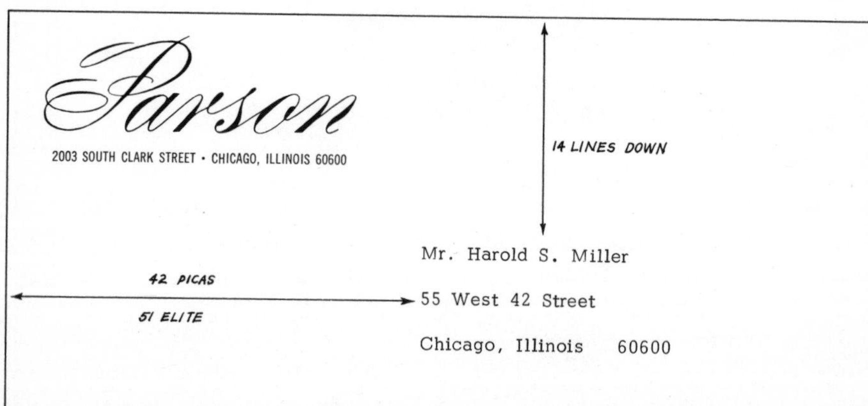

STANDARD-BLOCK STYLE LETTER

2003 SOUTH CLARK STREET • CHICAGO, ILLINOIS 60600 • TELEPHONE ANdover 4-7362

March 8, 19--

Mr. Harold S. Miller
55 West 42 Street
Chicago, Illinois 60600

Dear Mr. Miller:

Very truly yours,

PARSON

S. Cappy, Instructor

SC:hsp

Enc.

NOTES

NOTES

NOTES

NOTES

NOTES

NOTES

NOTES